I0796215

# EPIC BBQ SANDWICHES

## NEXT-LEVEL BURGERS, MELTS, SLIDERS, TACOS, AND MORE, GRILLED OR SMOKED TO PERFECTION

CREATOR OF CHILES AND SMOKE

**Quarto.com**



First Published in 2026 by The Harvard Common Press, an imprint of The Quarto Group, 100 Cummings Center, Suite 265-D, Beverly, MA 01915, USA. T (978) 282-9590 F (978) 283-2742

EEA Representation, WTS Tax d.o.o., Žanova ulica 3, 4000 Kranj, Slovenia. www.wts-tax.si



30 29 28 27 26 1 2 3 4 5

ISBN: 978-0-7603-9893-7

Digital edition published in 2026
eISBN: 978-0-7603-9894-4

Library of Congress Cataloging-in-Publication Data is available.

Design: Kelley Galbreath
Cover Images: Brad Prose
Photography: Brad Prose

Printed in Guangdong, China TT122025

# CONTENTS

## INTRODUCTION:

# SANDWICHES GRILLED, SMOKED, OR GRIDDLED

**OUR FRIDGE IS ALWAYS PACKED,** not with the basics but with the good stuff: smoked meats, tangy sauces, crunchy pickles, and all the little extras that make a meal unforgettable. I'm inspired every time I open that door, almost like I'm opening a storage box filled with LEGO sets. I see building blocks for something greater, and nothing brings all of those flavors together better than a sandwich.

I'm obsessed with sandwiches. They're not just a quick meal you slap together. They're a blank canvas for bold flavors, and honestly, one of the most satisfying ways to flex your creativity. Some of my earliest core food memories come from sandwiches I've had over the years. Some are cultural icons, some a little bit crazy: stuffed peanut-butter-French-toast, grilled Monte Cristos, and burgers with entire grilled cheese sandwiches as buns. Don't judge; I love to eat!

I've spent years diving deep into regional recipes, picking apart what makes them so irresistible, and then dragging them outside to my grill or smoker to see what kind of magic happens. From crispy bread to tangy sauces and smoky meats, sandwiches are where flavor gets to have a party. The best part? There are no rules. You can respect the traditions, then flip them on their head. And that's exactly what I love to do.

This book isn't about following rigid recipes or nailing "the perfect sandwich." It's about teaching you how to understand flavor, build texture, and, most importantly, how to use your grill or smoker to bring it all to life. It's about taking something as humble as a sandwich (even the classics) and exploring something new. I want you to feel confident tackling any recipe here, whether it's something you can throw together after work or a weekend project that leaves your grill crusted with smoky glory. Either way, it's worth it.

Sandwiches are my love language, and this book is full of everything I've learned: where to start, where to experiment, and where to throw the rules out completely. Let's fire up some meat, stack it high with bold flavors, and get ready to make your sandwich game legendary.

# HOW TO USE THIS BOOK

**THIS BOOK IS ALL ABOUT CREATING** the perfect sandwich by layering flavors and textures. We're talking thick slices of juicy brisket, crispy slaw, spicy sauces, and toasty breads. All the components that come together to deliver an experience with every bite. Because I live my life around smokers and grills, I wanted to take my barbecue obsession beyond the backyard and into the bun, showing you how to build sandwiches that hit all the right notes.

As you dive into this cookbook, the early recipes are simple enough to pull off in an afternoon, and the later recipes are more complex and challenging. I spent a lot of time thinking about how best to organize these recipes so you can start at the beginning and work your way through, coming out on the other side feeling like a true weekend warrior.

After all the sandwiches is a final chapter on breads, sauces, condiments, pickles, and more. You'll find useful stuff that'll help you build the ultimate sandwich. Some sandwich recipes will reference components or ingredients from this last chapter, so don't be surprised if you see them pop up more than once.

When I read cookbooks and see that there are unique sauce or condiment recipes, I don't want it to be a one-and-done situation. I want it to be something I can use over and over again, adding flavor to multiple dishes throughout the book. That's why I've made sure the recipes in this book work together so you can get the most out of the time you invest in each component. I want you to feel like every batch of sauce you make is totally worth it and will elevate a bunch of other meals too.

Now, there are no bread recipes in this book. I'm not a baker, as I mention in the discussion of breads later. But for every sandwich recipe, I'll point you toward the ideal bread and offer other great options along the way.

As you read through the book, keep an open mind. No recipe needs to be followed to the letter. You should feel empowered to make it your own!

1

# THE SANDWICH TOOLBOX

**YOU'LL BE SPENDING PLENTY OF TIME** outside while cooking your way through this book, and I'm here to make sure you enjoy every minute of it. All of these recipes can be cooked over a grill or in a smoker, with the occasional help from a blender. We all have our setup, and I want to give you the insight you need to succeed with what you've got.

## Grills and Smokers

Most of the grilling recipes in this book are geared toward charcoal grilling. Why? Because nothing beats the rich flavors that come from wood and fire. If you can, grab a charcoal grill that's big enough to set up a two-zone cooking area—hot coals on one side and a cooler zone on the other. This setup gives you ultimate control, with room to sear, smoke, rest, and even melt cheese.

If you're rocking a gas grill or cast-iron skillet, no worries—you can still tackle every recipe, just with a little less of that smoky goodness.

### CHARCOAL

When it comes to charcoal, go for high-quality briquettes or lump charcoal. Briquettes are great for maintaining a steady temperature and long burn times, which is perfect for smoking or slow cooking. Lump charcoal burns hotter and faster, producing less ash and giving off that natural wood flavor. Both are awesome options, and I've kept the recipes flexible enough for either.

### HARDWOOD

For that extra flavor boost, toss some wood chips or hardwood chunks into your charcoal grill. Many of the recipes in the book will use the cool zone of the

grill, so you've got time for that smoky infusion. Wood chips are great for short cooks, while hardwood chunks will give you a longer burn and more heat. Use your favorite wood. Oak, maple, apple, pecan, and hickory are all solid choices. Let that flavor shine.

**SMOKERS**

Both offset smokers and pellet grills are perfect for these recipes. As you dive deeper into the book, you'll find that the longer, more involved recipes really shine with an offset smoker. Some of the quicker recipes, though? They don't need a firebox. You can absolutely nail them with a pellet grill. Whether you're using an offset or a pellet grill, all of these barbecue recipes can be made with either style of smoker.

**GRIDDLES**

Many recipes in this book will make use of a griddle, and in some cases, it's actually a better choice than a cast-iron skillet. Having multiple cooking zones with a large, flat surface makes a huge difference, especially when you're trying to crisp up bacon, toast bread, and fry eggs all at once.

## Utensils and Tools

A solid utensil collection is more than just a great pair of grill tongs—although you *definitely* need those. (And by the way, remember to click them at least twice before touching any meat on the grill. It's required.)

Here's a list of the must-have tools and accessories I wouldn't dream of grilling or smoking without:

- **Tongs:** You'll need a few pairs of tongs, especially when you're dealing with raw meats: one for adding the meat to the grill, and another for flipping it. Make sure they're long enough to save your arm hair from getting singed.
- **Grilling gloves:** Gloves are essential when you're grilling. You want thick work gloves, not those flimsy plastic prep gloves. Trust me, thick gloves will come in handy when you need to pull food or hot pans off the grill or smoker.
- **Instant-read meat thermometer:** A quality thermometer is a game-changer. It takes the guesswork out of cooking and gives you confidence that you didn't just ruin the chicken. There's a big difference in quality, and it's worth investing in one that'll last.
- **Foil pans:** You'll go through a lot of foil pans if you're really into grilling and barbecue. They're dirt cheap in big box stores, and I always keep a stockpile, about 20 to 30 on hand at all times.

- **Heavy-duty foil:** Foil is a must-have for wrapping meat, covering foil pans, and general prep work. Make sure you've got plenty in your arsenal.
- **Pink butcher paper:** Only a few recipes call for butcher paper, but when you need it, you really need it—specifically for brisket. It helps hold in moisture and is ideal when you need to rest meats for a long period of time.
- **Blender or immersion blender:** A few recipes in this book will require making smooth sauces, and a blender is the tool you need. Stick or immersion blenders are perfect for this, and they can be used for any recipe that calls for blending.
- **Food processor:** A food processor is great when making salsas and sauces, especially when you don't want to completely puree the ingredients. It's perfect for chunky textures and mixing up those flavors.
- **Cast-iron skillet:** When you don't have a dedicated flattop-style griddle, grab a large skillet. This is ideal for some of the saucy recipes that require cooking down the meats with liquids for a period of time. You can use these over the coals or on the stove, it's up to you. Just make sure you preheat it slowly to temp before using.

- **Mandolin slicer:** Watch your fingers when using a mandolin—it has a way of sneaking up on you. While not a must-have, it's incredibly helpful for slicing cucumbers, onions, peppers, and more with precision and speed.

- **Baking sheet with wire rack:** You'll see this combo of baking sheet and wire rack come up a lot in the book. It's perfect for drying brining meats overnight in the fridge, and it's also great for keeping sandwiches warm in the oven. Just make sure the rack is elevated to allow for plenty of airflow.

- **Salad spinner:** A salad spinner is key for prepping salads and coleslaws. It's critical for getting crisp, fresh vegetables and skipping the soggy mess. Without one, you'll be stacking vegetables between paper towels, which isn't as fun as it sounds.

- **Mason jars:** These glass jars come in handy throughout the book for sauces, pickles, and more. Glass is perfect for pouring hot liquids into, unlike plastic deli containers that might not hold up as well. Plus, they just look cooler on your counter.

## Vacuum-Sealing

Leftover brisket? It sounds like a myth, but it happens. Especially if you're a smaller family with an eager beaver that just loves to barbecue. Trust me, from experience, it used to be hard to convince my wife that we needed a 16-pound (7.25 kg) whole packer brisket for the two of us. But once I got my hands on a vacuum sealer, everything changed.
If you're serious about barbecue or want to level up your meal prep game with smoked meats, a vacuum sealer is a game-changer. There are plenty of options out there at different price points, but the basics will do the trick when it comes to storing your smoked meats.

Vacuum-sealing keeps your meats juicy and actually boosts the smoke flavor. It's funny—sealing them in a bag with no oxygen lets the flavors intensify, especially if you let the meat sit in the fridge for a few days before digging in.

The only downside? Some of that crispy bark will be softened when you open the bag. But don't sweat it! You can typically restore the bark by warming the meat back up in your smoker.

Here are a few tips to bring your slowly smoked meat back to life:

- **Seal before slicing:** If you can, seal the meat before slicing it. Larger cuts of smoked meat stay juicier and are easier to bring back to life, especially when you're recrisping that bark.

- **Reheat in water:** If you've got shredded or sliced meat, warm the still-sealed bag gently in a simmering pot of water. This takes about 15 to 20 minutes, depending on the size of the bag. Bring the water to a boil, then drop in the bag and reduce the heat to a simmer. If you want to help things along, cover the pot to steam the bag. Once it's hot, open it up and sear, shred, or slice the meat however you like.

- **Warm in a cast-iron skillet:** For sliced meats like smoked turkey or brisket, just heat up the slices in a cast-iron skillet on medium-low. This slow warming will keep the texture intact while you get that perfect sear on the outside. And if you're feeling bold, crank up the heat and let it rip for a bit of that crispy char!

# 2

# WEEKNIGHT HERO: CASUAL AND EASY SANDWICHES

# SMOKY CHEESY JOE

**SERVES ABOUT 6**
**EQUIPMENT: SMOKER AND SKILLET**

- 1½ pounds (680 g) ground beef, 85/15 recommended
- 2 tablespoons (26 g) Prime Smoke Rub (p. 173)
- 1 tablespoon (15 ml) avocado oil
- 1 sweet onion, diced
- 2 tablespoons (18 g) minced chipotles in adobo
- 2 garlic cloves, minced
- 1 teaspoon ground cumin
- 1 can (15 ounces [444 ml]) tomato sauce
- 12 ounces (355 ml) beer, such as Mexican lager
- 1 tablespoon (15 ml) Worcestershire sauce
- Salt and coarsely ground black pepper to taste
- 6 burger buns (see bread recommendations)
- Softened butter, for toasting
- 2 cups (473 ml) Creamy Cheese Sauce (p. 166)
- Pickled Jalapeños (p. 182)

**BREAD RECOMMENDATIONS:**

- Portuguese rolls
- Telera rolls
- Potato buns
- Onion rolls

**You are not too old for this sandwich. This kicked-up sloppy joe is not one to be overlooked. Smoked ground beef is seared with a savory, spicy combo of garlic, chipotles, and beer, creating a thick, rich meat sauce. Pile that onto grilled buns and blanket it with homemade cheese sauce—trust me. And make sure you eat this sandwich over a pile of corn chips, because everything that falls off makes instant nachos.**

**1.** Preheat the smoker to 225°F (107°C). This recipe works best with a pellet smoker, but you can also use a two-zone setup on a charcoal grill to smoke the beef portions.

**2.** Divide the ground beef into 4 large portions, pressing just enough to hold their shape. Dust the beef with the seasoning on all sides, then place it in the smoker. Let it cook for 30 to 35 minutes until the outside develops a brick-red color. Remove the beef and get ready to sear.

**3.** Heat up the avocado oil in a large skillet over medium-low heat over the hot coals or a stove. Add the diced onions, cooking for 2 to 3 minutes until softened. Add in the chipotles, garlic, and cumin, stirring and cooking for an additional 2 minutes before adding in the smoked ground beef. Press the beef into the skillet, searing the portions and then breaking them up to brown evenly.

**4.** Cook the beef down for a few minutes, then add the tomato sauce, beer, and Worcestershire. Mix everything well and simmer uncovered for about 10 to 15 minutes until the meat sauce has thickened. Taste and adjust with salt and pepper as needed.

**5.** Remove the skillet from the heat. Toast the buns with butter on the grill grates, if desired. Serve the sandwiches on the buns with Creamy Cheese Sauce and Pickled Jalapeños.

# SANTA MARIA TRI-TIP

**MAKES 4 SANDWICHES**
**EQUIPMENT: CHARCOAL GRILL**

1 whole tri-tip, about 2 to 3 pounds (907 g to 1.4 kg)

2 tablespoons (30 ml) Worcestershire sauce

3 tablespoons (39 g) Prime Smoke Rub (p. 173), plus more as needed

3 Anaheim chiles

1 bunch scallions (for the aioli)

Charred Scallion Aioli (p. 80)

Tomatoes, sliced

4 rolls (see bread recommendations)

**BREAD RECOMMENDATIONS:**

Bolillo rolls

French rolls

Hoagie rolls

Ciabatta

**This California classic is all about seriously tender, juicy beef slices piled high with fresh toppings like roasted peppers, salsas, tomatoes, and maybe even some melty cheese. We cook tri-tip more than any other beef cut—it's a total juice bomb and perfect for stacking into sandwiches or tacos. I'm not one to waste hot coals, so I take this recipe up a notch by charring scallions for a killer aioli and roasting Anaheim chiles to add that fresh heat to every bite. Soft bolillo rolls soak up all the juices and make the perfect handheld, packed with that delicious wood-fired flavor. You'll be so full, you might just need a nap . . . or at least, it's a solid excuse to loosen the pants.**

**1.** Trim the tri-tip by removing any excess fat or silverskin. Brush it with Worcestershire sauce and season it thoroughly on all sides. Set it aside to rest while you prepare the charcoal grill for two-zone cooking. Once the coals are hot, move them to one side of the grill, close the lid, and allow the grill to reach temperature, aiming for about 300°F (149°C).

**2.** Toss the Anaheim chiles, along with the scallions for the aioli, on the grill. The scallions will char up fast, so keep an eye on them and pull them off once they've got some solid grill marks. Let the chiles keep cooking until they're charred on all sides, then place them into a sealed container for about 10 minutes—this allows you to easily remove the charred skins and seeds. Slice the skinned chiles into thin strips for the sandwiches.

**3.** Place the steak on the cool side of the grill, away from the coals. Position the thickest part closest to the fire so the thinner side doesn't overcook. Close the lid and let the tri-tip cook for about 45 to 60 minutes, or until it hits around 118°F to 120°F (48°C to 49°C).

CONTINUED →

## SANTA MARIA TRI-TIP, CONTINUED

**4.** While the tri-tip is smoking, make the Charred Scallion Aioli. Trim the ends of the scallions and roughly chop them. Throw all the ingredients into a small food processor and give it a quick blitz until smooth. Taste and adjust with salt and black pepper if needed. Set it aside in the fridge until you're ready to serve.

**5.** Slice the tomato and lay the slices on a paper towel. Sprinkle them with salt to draw out the excess moisture and enhance the flavor. Let them sit for at least 10 minutes, then pat them dry with the towel.

**6.** Once the tri-tip hits your target temperature, take the lid off the grill and let the coals heat up to a nice, hot glow for searing. Move the steak over to the hot side and sear for about a minute per side, flipping it until the internal temperature reaches around 128°F to 130°F (53°C to 54°C) for that perfect medium-rare. Pull it off the grill and let it rest for 15 minutes. Slice only when you're ready to serve to keep all that juice locked in. You'll likely have some leftover tri-tip after making the sandwiches, which is just a bonus.

**7.** Cut open a bolillo roll and slather on some of that aioli. Layer in the tomato slices, thinly sliced steak, and grilled chile strips. I like to sprinkle a little more of the beef seasoning on top to finish it off. Press that sandwich together, take a big bite, and enjoy the flavor explosion.

# KICKIN' CHICKEN BREAKFAST

**MAKES 4 SANDWICHES**
**EQUIPMENT: CHARCOAL GRILL AND SKILLET**

**FOR MARINADE:**

- 4 boneless and skinless chicken breast fillets
- 1½ tablespoons (22 ml) avocado oil
- 1 tablespoon (9 g) minced chipotles in adobo
- 2 teaspoons kosher salt
- 1 teaspoon paprika
- ½ teaspoon celery salt
- ½ teaspoon granulated garlic
- ½ teaspoon coarsely ground black pepper
- ½ teaspoon cayenne powder

**FOR HOT HONEY MUSTARD SAUCE:**

- ¼ cup (60 g) Fresh Mayonnaise (p. 157)
- ¼ cup (44 g) Dijon mustard
- ¼ cup (85 g) Hot Honey (p. 171)
- 2 tablespoons (30 ml) apple cider vinegar
- Salt to taste

- 8 slices bacon
- 4 eggs
- 4 buns or biscuits (see bread recommendations)
- American cheese
- Pickled Jalapeños (p. 182), optional

**Every Thursday morning at my old call center job, the cafeteria had a breakfast special they called Kickin' Chicken: a small fried chicken fillet, hot sauce, cheese, and a fried egg. Let me tell you—this sandwich got me through some seriously stressful days, and I never forgot its power. This juicy chicken breast is marinated in a mix of spices and chiles for a zippy heat, paired with crispy bacon, melty cheese that blends into the rich egg, and a hot honey mustard sauce to tie it all together. One bite, and your morning problems will disappear.**

**1.** Grab a large resealable bag and lay the chicken flat inside—this will become your marinade bag. Take a skillet or a heavy pan and gently smack them into an even thickness, roughly ½-inch (1-cm) thick—this helps them cook evenly on the grill. If your chicken breasts are super thick, no need to smack—just slice them in half lengthwise to create thinner fillets. For smaller breasts, butterflying them works just as well.

**2.** Mix the oil, chipotles, kosher salt, paprika, celery salt, garlic, black pepper, and cayenne together in a small bowl. Stir it all together, then pour the marinade into the bag with the chicken. Gently massage the bag to coat the chicken evenly. Squeeze out as much air as you can and seal it up, letting the chicken marinate for 1 to 2 hours.

**3.** Combine the ingredients for the Hot Honey Mustard Sauce, adjusting with salt to taste.

**4.** Preheat the grill for two-zone cooking by banking the coals to one side, aiming for a temperature around 400°F (204°C). Clean the grates. Remove the chicken from the marinade and place it directly over the coals to sear. After about 2 to 3 minutes, flip the chicken—it should release easily from the grates—and sear the other side for another 2 to 3 minutes. Move the chicken to the cooler side of the grill.

CONTINUED →

## KICKIN' CHICKEN BREAKFAST, CONTINUED

**BREAD RECOMMENDATIONS:**

Croissants

Brioche buns

English muffins

Buttermilk biscuits

Kaiser rolls

**5.** Place a cast-iron skillet over the coals and add the bacon strips to the pan. Cook slowly, flipping as needed until it crisps up. Once crispy, remove the bacon and set it aside to drain on a paper towel.

**6.** Drop the eggs into the skillet, carefully spooning the hot bacon fat over the egg whites until they're no longer jiggly. Cook the eggs to your preferred doneness, then remove them from the pan.

**7.** Toast the buns or biscuits in the remaining bacon fat for about a minute, until golden brown. Remove the skillet from the grill.

**8.** Check the temperature of the chicken breasts, then close the lid, leaving the vents slightly open for indirect cooking. Let the chicken cook for another 10 to 15 minutes, or until it reaches 160°F to 162°F (71°C to 72°C). Remove from the grill, top with slices of American cheese, and let it rest. The cheese will melt while the chicken comes up to a safe 165°F (74°C).

**9.** Start with the bottom bun, dollop on some of the sauce, add the bacon, chicken, egg, and top with the other bun. If you want a little extra heat and zing, Pickled Jalapeños are the perfect addition.

## Make Ahead, Save Time

Leftover roast beef is perfect for making delicious sandwiches all week. Cook the beef using the recipe, let it cool slightly, then vacuum-seal and store it whole in the fridge. Avoid slicing it before storing to keep all those delicious juices locked in. When you're ready to eat, slice it up as needed. Your roast will stay fresh for 3 to 5 days.

# PIT BEEF 'N' CHEDDAR

**MAKES 8 SANDWICHES**
**EQUIPMENT: CHARCOAL GRILL**

---

3-pound (1.36-kg) top round or eye of round roast

2 tablespoons (30 ml) Worcestershire sauce

3 tablespoons (39 g) Prime Smoke Rub (p. 173)

**FOR HORSERADISH SAUCE:**

½ cup (115 g) sour cream

2 tablespoons (30 g) prepared horseradish, drained

2 tablespoons (28 g) Fresh Mayonnaise (p. 157)

1 tablespoon (15 ml) freshly squeezed lemon juice

1 tablespoon (3 g) chives, finely diced

Coarsely ground black pepper and salt to taste

2 cups (473 ml) Creamy Cheese Sauce (p. 166)

Softened butter, for toasting

8 buns (see bread recommendations)

**BREAD RECOMMENDATIONS:**

Buttermilk buns

Onion buns

Kaiser rolls

Pretzel buns

**As a kid, I was hooked on a certain roast beef and cheddar sandwich from a drive-thru we won't name (but you probably know). That combo of tender beef and melty cheese sauce was my jam. Over time, I discovered the Baltimore pit beef sandwich and realized that roast beef could be *so much better.* Think rare, juicy beef with a perfect sear, homemade cheddar sauce, and a creamy horseradish kick to tie it all together. It's everything little me loved—just grown-up and way more epic.**

**1.** Preheat the grill for two-zone cooking, banking the hot coals to one side. Aim for about 250°F to 275°F (121°C to 135°C). Add wood chunks for additional smoke flavor, such as oak or hickory.

**2.** Brush the beef with the Worcestershire sauce as a binder, and roll it in the seasoning to cover all sides generously. Don't skimp on the seasoning, as this is a thicker cut of beef. Place it on the grill's cool side, allowing it to smoke slowly for 45 minutes, or until it reaches about 115°F (46°C) internal temperature.

**3.** Mix the ingredients for the Horseradish Sauce, seasoning with salt and pepper to taste.

**4.** When the beef nears your target temperature, remove the grill lid to let the coals fire up for searing. Sear the beef for about a minute per side, rotating every minute until it develops a crust and hits your desired temperature. Pull the roast at 120°F (49°C) for rare or around 130°F (54°C) for medium-rare, then let it rest.

**5.** Prepare the Creamy Cheese Sauce while the meat is resting. Butter the buns and place them on the grill briefly to toast them while the coals are still hot.

**6.** Once the meat has rested, thinly slice it and serve while warm. Assemble the sandwich by adding a dollop of the Horseradish Sauce, piling on the juicy beef, and topping with the Creamy Cheese Sauce. Have a napkin or two handy; you'll need it.

# FAJITA SMASH BURGERS

**MAKES 4 LARGE BURGERS**
**EQUIPMENT: GRIDDLE OR SKILLET**

**FOR MARINATED PEPPERS AND ONIONS:**

2 poblano peppers, seeded and thinly sliced

2 red bell peppers, seeded and thinly sliced

1 jalapeño pepper, thinly sliced into rings

½ sweet onion, thinly sliced

1 tablespoon (15 ml) avocado oil

Juice of 2 fresh limes

1 teaspoon kosher salt

2 tablespoons (30 ml) Worcestershire sauce

24 ounces (680 g) ground beef, 80/20, divided into 3-ounce (85 g) portions

4 hamburger buns (see bread recommendations)

Softened butter, for toasting

3 tablespoons (39 g) Prime Smoke Rub (p. 173)

4 slices Havarti, Monterey Jack, or white American cheese

Lime wedges

Sour Cream Sandwich Sauce (p. 159)

**BREAD RECOMMENDATIONS:**

Potato buns

Sesame buns

Brioche buns

Buttermilk buns

Tortas

**My wife is always asking me to sear up marinated peppers and onions for the week. And honestly, there's no reason to waste a hot skillet when I'm always looking for an excuse to smash some burgers. While I love traditional fajitas, there's something special about biting into a crusty smashed burger, paired with tangy peppers, sweet onions, and creamy sauce.**

**1.** Combine the peppers and onion in a resealable bag. Add the avocado oil, lime juice, and salt. Seal the bag tightly, pressing out as much air as possible, and give it a good mix with your hands to coat everything. Pop the bag in the fridge and let those flavors marinate for at least 2 hours, or even overnight.

**2.** When you're ready to sear the burgers, pull the peppers and onions out of the fridge. Preheat a cast-iron skillet or griddle over medium heat. Add Worcestershire sauce to the ground beef and mix with your hands to incorporate. Shape the ground beef into 4 balls and get ready to sear.

**3.** Add the peppers and onions to the hot skillet, letting them sear for 1 to 2 minutes before stirring. Cook for about 5 to 6 minutes, or until they reach your preferred softness, then set them aside in a bowl for serving.

**4.** Toast the buns in the same skillet, soaking up the leftover oil from the peppers and onions. If needed, add a little butter to help build that golden, crispy crust.

**5.** Drop a ball of ground beef onto the hot skillet and smash it flat with a burger press or metal spatula. Sprinkle generously with seasoning right away. If there's enough space on your skillet or griddle, add more beef and repeat. Let the burgers sear for about 2 minutes, then scrape underneath with a spatula and flip. Top with sliced cheese of choice, turn the heat down to low to avoid overcooking, and stack the burgers when ready. Place them on the toasted buns for serving.

**6.** Squeeze a little lime on the peppers and onions before stacking them high on the burger. Slather a dollop of sour cream sauce on the bun, smash it all together, and dig in!

# CAJUN CHICKEN SANDWICH

**MAKES 8 SANDWICHES**
**EQUIPMENT: CHARCOAL GRILL**

**FOR MARINADE:**

1½ tablespoons (22 ml) olive oil

2 small garlic cloves, minced or pressed through a garlic press

1 sprig fresh thyme

¼ cup (59 ml) Louisiana-style hot sauce

½ tablespoon (1 g) smoked paprika

½ teaspoon dried oregano

½ teaspoon kosher salt

½ teaspoon coarsely ground black pepper

1 tablespoon (15 ml) Worcestershire sauce

8 boneless, skinless chicken thighs

**FOR REMOULADE:**

1 cup (225 g) Fresh Mayonnaise (p. 157)

2 tablespoons (22 g) grainy or Creole mustard

1 clove garlic, minced

2 tablespoons (30 g) prepared horseradish, plus more as needed

1 teaspoon Worcestershire sauce

2 teaspoons lemon juice

½ teaspoon paprika

½ teaspoon cayenne pepper, plus more as needed

1 tablespoon (4 g) chopped fresh parsley

**FOR HORSERADISH PICKLE SLAW:**

½ head green cabbage, finely shredded on a mandolin or by hand

3 tablespoons (54 g) kosher salt

2 tablespoons (26 g) white sugar

½ cup (113 g) prepared Remoulade, plus more as needed

Sliced Pickled Okra (p. 185) or preferred pickles to taste

Salt and coarsely ground black pepper to taste

Louisiana-style hot sauce to taste

Tomatoes, sliced

8 buns (see bread recommendations)

Softened butter, for toasting

Louisiana-style hot sauce

**BREAD RECOMMENDATIONS:**

Potato rolls

Kaiser rolls

French bread

French rolls

Baguette

Cajun flavors and charcoal grilling go hand in hand—adding that kiss of wood-fired smoke makes all the difference. Spicy, marinated chicken hits the grill, paired with a crispy, pickled slaw that packs a punch with horseradish and spicy mustard. Every layer of this sandwich brings out the best in each ingredient, making it nearly impossible to put down. This recipe is a great template if you want to swap in chicken breasts or change up the bread style. And of course, make sure you've got plenty of Louisiana-style hot sauce on hand.

**1.** Prepare the marinade by adding all of the ingredients except the chicken to a bowl and stirring to combine. Place the chicken thighs in a large resealable bag and pour in the marinade. Gently massage the bag to coat the chicken evenly. Squeeze out as much air as you can and seal it up, letting the chicken marinate for 1 to 2 hours.

**2.** Combine the ingredients for the remoulade, taste, and adjust. Add more horseradish or cayenne for extra heat. Store in the fridge until ready to use.

CONTINUED →

## CAJUN CHICKEN SANDWICH, CONTINUED

**3.** For the slaw, combine the shredded cabbage with the salt and sugar in a large bowl, tossing to coat. Let it rest for 5 minutes, then transfer it to a colander and rinse under cold running water. Dry the cabbage with a salad spinner, or layer it between paper towels on a baking sheet to blot dry. Return the cabbage to the large bowl and add ½ cup of the Remoulade, tossing to coat. Add as much as you like, depending on how wet you prefer your slaw. Stir in the sliced Pickled Okra or pickles of choice and toss to combine. Taste and adjust with salt, black pepper, or a bit more hot sauce. Store in the fridge until ready to serve.

**4.** Salt the tomato slices lightly on both sides and press them between some paper towels, letting them sit for at least 10 minutes to drain off some of the excess liquid.

**5.** Preheat the grill for two-zone cooking by banking the coals to one side, aiming for a temperature around 400°F (204°C). Clean the grates. Remove the chicken from the marinade and place it directly over the coals to sear. After about 2 to 3 minutes, flip the chicken—it should release easily from the grates—and sear the other side for another 2 to 3 minutes. Move the chicken to the cooler side of the grill, close the lid, and leave the vents slightly open for indirect cooking. Let the chicken cook for another 15 to 20 minutes, or until it reaches 175°F to 180°F (79°C to 82°C).

**6.** Remove the chicken from the grill once it reaches the target temperature and let it rest while you toast the buns. Butter the buns and place them on the grill briefly to toast them while the coals are still hot. It only takes a minute—don't burn the bread!

**7.** Assemble the sandwiches by spreading some leftover Remoulade on the bottom bun, followed by a slice of tomato, grilled chicken, and the slaw. Add a dash of hot sauce, then top with the other bun before digging in.

**Note:** Chicken thighs should be cooked to a higher temperature than chicken breasts, which helps improve their tenderness. The extra fat in thighs needs that additional time and heat to render down, making them more juicy and flavorful.

# SWEET AND SPICY THAI CHICKEN

**MAKES 8 SANDWICHES**
**EQUIPMENT: CHARCOAL GRILL**

**FOR MARINADE:**

- 1 large lemongrass stalk
- 2 tablespoons (30 ml) neutral oil
- 6 cloves garlic, minced
- 2 tablespoons (30 ml) lime juice
- 1 jalapeño pepper, thinly sliced into rounds
- 3 tablespoons (44 ml) fish sauce
- 3 tablespoons (44ml) soy sauce
- 1 tablespoon (15 g) brown sugar
- ½ tablespoon coarsely ground black pepper
- 8 boneless, skinless chicken thighs

**FOR ASIAN SLAW:**

- ½ small red cabbage, finely shredded on a mandolin or by hand
- 1 tablespoon (18 g) plus 1 teaspoon kosher salt, divided, plus more as needed
- 1 medium carrot, peeled and thinly sliced into rounds
- 1 English cucumber, thinly sliced into rounds
- 1 jalapeño pepper, thinly sliced into rounds
- ½ cup (8 g) cilantro leaves
- 3 tablespoons (44 ml) rice wine vinegar
- 1 tablespoon (13 g) white sugar

- 8 buns (see bread recommendations)
- Softened butter, for toasting
- Kewpie mayo

**BREAD RECOMMENDATIONS:**

- Sesame buns
- Baguette
- French bread
- Hoagie rolls

**Sometimes, you just want a fresh sandwich with some crispy veggies and that's exactly what this one's all about. Juicy marinated chicken thighs grilled over charcoal pair perfectly with a crunchy, refreshing slaw that brings the right amount of bite. Add a dollop of Kewpie mayo—savory, sweet, and creamy—to tie it all together. It's fresh, it's crunchy, and it's got just the right kick. This sandwich will hit the spot.**

**1.** Remove the dried outer leaves from the lemongrass. Use the back of a chef's knife to smack the root end, which helps release the tough outer layer and bruise it to release its essential oils. Slice off the roots, dice the smashed stalk, and add it to a bowl.

**2.** Add the rest of the marinade ingredients to the bowl and stir to combine. Place the chicken thighs in a large resealable bag and pour in the marinade. Gently massage the bag to coat the chicken evenly. Squeeze out as much air as you can, seal the bag, and let the chicken marinate for 1 to 2 hours.

**3.** For the slaw, combine the shredded cabbage with 1 tablespoon (18 g) kosher salt in a large bowl, tossing to coat. Let it rest for 5 minutes, then transfer it to a colander and rinse under cold running water. Dry the cabbage with a

CONTINUED →

## SWEET AND SPICY THAI CHICKEN, CONTINUED

salad spinner, or layer it between paper towels on a baking sheet to blot dry. Return the cabbage to the large bowl and add the carrot, cucumber, jalapeño, cilantro, vinegar, sugar, and 1 teaspoon kosher salt, tossing gently to combine. Taste, and adjust with more salt if needed. Store in an airtight container in the fridge until ready to serve.

**4.** Preheat the grill for two-zone cooking by banking the coals to one side, aiming for a temperature around 400°F (204°C). Clean the grates and remove the chicken from the marinade. Do not discard the marinade; it will become a sauce.

**5.** Place the chicken on the grill, directly over the coals to sear. After about 2 to 3 minutes, flip the chicken—it should release easily from the grates—and sear the other side for another 2 to 3 minutes. Move the chicken to the cooler side of the grill, close the lid, and leave the vents slightly open for indirect cooking. Let the chicken cook for another 15 to 20 minutes, or until it reaches 175°F to 180°F (79°C to 82°C).

**6.** While the chicken is cooking, strain the marinade and add the reserved liquid to a small saucepan. Bring the liquid to a boil over medium heat, then reduce the heat and simmer until it's reduced by half, about 10 minutes. It should be a syruplike consistency that coats the back of a spoon. Turn off the heat and set the sauce aside—it'll be used to drizzle over the chicken.

**7.** Remove the chicken from the grill once it reaches the target temperature and let it rest while you toast the buns. Butter the buns and place them on the grill briefly to toast them while the coals are still hot.

**8.** Assemble the sandwiches by spreading some of the Kewpie mayo on the bottom bun, followed by the grilled chicken, slaw, and a drizzle of that reduced sauce. Top with the second bun and bite into your fresh, crunchy, savory chicken sandwich.

# HONEY PEPPER PIMENTO CHICKEN

**MAKES 4 SANDWICHES**
**EQUIPMENT: CHARCOAL GRILL**

**FOR MARINADE:**

2 teaspoons kosher salt

2 teaspoons coarsely ground black pepper

1½ teaspoons paprika

1 teaspoon garlic powder

2 tablespoons (30 ml) pickle juice

1 tablespoon (15 ml) neutral oil

4 boneless and skinless chicken breast fillets, 6 to 8 ounces each (170 to 227 g)

**FOR PIMENTO CHEESE SPREAD:**

8 ounces (227 g) cream cheese, softened

½ cup (115 g) Fresh Mayonnaise (p. 157)

2 cups (225 g) freshly grated cheddar cheese

½ teaspoon paprika

½ teaspoon ground mustard

½ teaspoon white sugar

¼ teaspoon freshly ground black pepper

4 ounces (113 g) jarred pimentos, drained

Salt and coarsely ground black pepper to taste

Hot Honey (p. 171)

Butter

8 slices of bread or 4 rolls (see bread recommendations)

Pickled Jalapeños (p. 182)

**BREAD RECOMMENDATIONS:**

Texas toast

White bread

Pullman loaf

Potato rolls

Sesame buns

**If you're looking for an excuse to treat yourself, this is the sandwich to do it with. Start by grabbing the sandwich and give that toasted, pillowy Texas toast a little press to soak up all the juicy goodness. The sides of the bread buckle in, folding over the smoky grilled chicken and creamy pimento cheese. Don't cheap out on the bread for this sandwich because it becomes the star as it soaks up all of the chicken juices, honey, and pickle brine. Hungry yet? Just wait 'til you smell this, it's irresistible.**

**1.** Grab a large resealable bag and lay the chicken flat inside—this will become your marinade bag. Take a skillet or a heavy pan and gently smack them into an even thickness, roughly ½-inch (1-cm) thick—this helps them cook evenly on the grill. If your chicken breasts are super thick, no need to smack—just slice them in half lengthwise to create thinner fillets. For smaller breasts, butterflying them works just as well.

**2.** Mix the salt, black pepper, paprika, and garlic powder in a small bowl with the pickle juice and oil. Stir it all together, then pour the marinade into the bag with the chicken. Gently massage the bag to coat the chicken evenly. Squeeze out as much air as you can and seal it up, letting the chicken marinate for 1 to 2 hours.

**CONTINUED** →

## HONEY PEPPER PIMENTO CHICKEN, CONTINUED

**3.** Add all of the Pimento Cheese Spread ingredients in a large bowl, leaving out the pimento peppers for now. Use a wooden spoon to incorporate all of the creamy flavors together. Once it's fairly smooth, gently fold in the pimentos. Taste it and adjust with more salt and pepper if needed. Pop it in the fridge while the chicken marinates.

**4.** Preheat the grill for two-zone cooking by banking the coals to one side, aiming for a temperature around 400°F (204°C). Clean the grates. Remove the chicken from the marinade and place it directly over the coals to sear. After about 2 to 3 minutes, flip the chicken—it should release easily from the grates—and sear the other side for another 2 to 3 minutes. Move the chicken to the cooler side of the grill, close the lid, and leave the vents slightly open for indirect cooking. Let the chicken cook for another 15 to 20 minutes, or until it reaches 160°F to 162°F (71°C to 72°C).

**5.** Remove the chicken and allow it to rest for a few minutes before serving. While it's still warm, drizzle some of the Hot Honey over the chicken to let it soak in.

**6.** Heat up a pan on the stove with a little butter, and toast the bread until it's golden perfection. Smear the Pimento Cheese Spread on the bottom slice, top it with the honey-glazed chicken and Pickled Jalapeños, then finish it off with the top slice. Maybe add a little extra Hot Honey—go ahead, you've earned it.

# SMOKED PASTRAMI STEAK

**MAKES 4 SANDWICHES**
**EQUIPMENT: CHARCOAL GRILL OR SMOKER**

1 whole tri-tip, about 2 to 3 pounds (907 g to 1.4 kg)

3 tablespoons Pastrami Spice Rub (recipe below), plus more as needed

**FOR PASTRAMI SPICE RUB:**

3 tablespoons (15 g) black peppercorns

2 tablespoons (10 g) coriander seeds

½ teaspoon fennel seeds

1 tablespoon (15 g) brown sugar

1 teaspoon paprika

1 teaspoon granulated garlic

½ teaspoon chili flakes

**FOR SPICY DIJONNAISE:**

½ cup (115 g) Fresh Mayonnaise (p. 157)

2 tablespoons (22 g) Dijon mustard

Juice of ½ lemon

2 tablespoons (30 ml) prepared horseradish

Salt to taste

Softened butter, for toasting

8 slices bread (see bread recommendations)

Horseradish Slaw (p. 168) or sauerkraut

4 slices Gouda cheese

**BREAD RECOMMENDATIONS:**

Jewish rye bread

Caraway rye bread

Thin-sliced sourdough

French baguette

**Note:** You may add hardwood chunks for additional smoke flavors, such as maple, apple, or pecan wood for mild flavors. Avoid woods such as mesquite or hickory that will overpower the pastrami spices.

Homemade pastrami is incredibly delicious—but it's a lot of work. I don't always have the fridge space or patience to brine a whole brisket for a week. This method of smoking a steak to mimic the classic pastrami flavors is my way of getting the taste I love without the long wait. While it skips the briny flavor, this method is absolutely worth it. Paired with spicy Dijonnaise, zesty slaw, and rich Gouda, this sandwich deserves its own spotlight. That's why it's in the book—you need this.

**1.** Trim the tri-tip by removing any excess fat or silverskin. Use a spice grinder to coarsely grind the peppercorns, coriander seeds, and fennel seeds. Mix the ground spices together with the other ingredients for the pastrami seasoning. Generously season the tri-tip on all sides, and place it on a baking sheet with a wire rack in the fridge for at least 2 hours, up to overnight. This step will dry out the surface, allowing for more smoke penetration and a crispier crust—key characteristics for pastrami.

**2.** Take the tri-tip out of the fridge when it's time to cook. Prepare the charcoal grill for two-zone cooking, aiming for about 300°F (149°C). Once the coals are hot, move them to one side of the grill, close the lid, and allow the grill to reach temperature.

CONTINUED →

## SMOKED PASTRAMI STEAK, CONTINUED

**3.** Place the meat on the cool side of the grill, away from the coals. Position the thickest part closest to the fire so the thinner side doesn't overcook. Close the lid and let the tri-tip cook for about 45 to 60 minutes, or until it hits around 118°F to 120°F (48°C to 49°C).

**4.** While the tri-tip is smoking, prepare the Spicy Dijonnaise by combining the mayonnaise, Dijon, lemon juice, and prepared horseradish. Taste and adjust with salt if needed.

**5.** Once the tri-tip hits your target temperature, take the lid off the grill and let the coals heat up to a nice, hot glow for searing. Move the meat over to the hot side and sear for about a minute per side, flipping it until the internal temperature reaches around 128°F to 130°F (53°C to 54°C) for that perfect medium-rare. Pull it off the grill and let it rest for 15 minutes. Slice only when you're ready to serve to keep all that juice locked in.

**6.** Spread the butter onto the bread and grill for 1 minute, or until toasted. If your grill is too hot, you can use a cast-iron skillet—melt the butter in the pan, then add the bread. Cook until the bread is golden and crispy.

**7.** Build the sandwich by spreading some of the sauce on the bottom slice of bread, followed by a generous amount of thinly sliced beef, slaw or sauerkraut, a slice of cheese, and another sauced slice of bread. I like to place the sandwich back on the cool side of the grill for 2 minutes, which helps melt the cheese. Don't waste those coals!

## Slow-Smoked, Fast Feasts

**SMOKING BARBECUE AFTER** a long day might seem like a weekend-only gig, but it doesn't have to be. Who says you can't enjoy incredible smoked meats during the week? I'm here to show you how to make it happen. Be sure to check out the vacuum-sealing section (p. 13) for tips on how to store and restore your barbecue.

Throughout this book, you'll find a few sections dedicated to smoking meats in advance—so you've always got flavorful options to layer between toasty bread. I'll cover a few staple barbecue cooks such as smoked pulled chicken (p. 41), smoked turkey breast (p. 78), and yes—smoked brisket (p. 119).

Because let's be real, one of the best things about barbecue is enjoying it beyond the big cookout. Whether it's sneaking a bite late at night or grabbing a smoked chicken salad sandwich for lunch, this book's got you covered.

# SMOKED PULLED CHICKEN

**SERVES ABOUT 4 TO 5**
**EQUIPMENT: SMOKER**

- 1 whole chicken, about 4 to 6 pounds (1.8 to 2.7 kg)
- ¼ cup seasoning of choice, plus more as needed

**Note:** It's optional, but I highly recommend dry-brining the chicken overnight on a baking sheet with a wire rack, uncovered in the fridge. The circulating air helps dry out the skin, and the salt works its magic, getting deeper into the meat and skin. Plus, it boosts smoke penetration—definitely a win all around!

**This is a regular in our house almost every week. Having smoked chicken ready for sandwiches, wraps, or tacos is a huge time-saver for meal prep, and honestly, it tastes way better than those store-bought rotisserie chickens. Flattening the chicken helps it cook evenly and soak up more smoke flavor, and it cuts down on the cooking time. It's a win all around. Use this juicy meat for the sandwich ideas covered in the next few pages.**

**1.** Use kitchen shears to remove the chicken's backbone. Flip it over so the bones are facing down, then press firmly on the breastbone to snap it and flatten the chicken. Generously season all sides with the seasoning. Let it rest, uncovered, in the fridge for at least 30 minutes before cooking.

**2.** Remove the chicken from the fridge. Let it rest at room temperature while the smoker preheats. Set the smoker to 265°F to 275°F (129°C to 135°C). Place the chicken in the smoker, bone-side down, and cook for about 90 minutes, or until the breast reaches 165°F to 170°F (74°C to 77°C) and the thighs hit 185°F to 190°F (85°C to 88°C).

**3.** Take the chicken off the smoker and place it in a large nonreactive bowl or foil pan. Cover it with plastic wrap and let it steam for about 20 minutes while it cools. This will make shredding the chicken a whole lot easier.

**4.** Remove the meat from the bones and skin, shredding it into evenly sized pieces. Rub some of the crispy skin into the meat to transfer that seasoning and fat, then give it a taste. Depending on what you're using it for, you might want to add a little more seasoning to dial in the flavor.

**5.** Keep the chicken warm if you're using it to make sandwiches, such as the White Chicken Enchilada Roll (p. 42) or the Nashville Hot Chicken Melt (p. 45). Store the smoked pulled chicken in a sealed container, which will stay fresh in the fridge for about 4 to 5 days.

# WHITE CHICKEN ENCHILADA ROLL

**MAKES 4 SANDWICHES**
**EQUIPMENT: SMOKER AND OVEN**

1 recipe Smoked Pulled Chicken (p. 41)

1 tablespoon (8 g) chili powder, plus more as needed

¼ cup (36 g) diced green or Hatch chiles

**FOR CHEESE SAUCE:**

3 tablespoons (43 g) butter

3 tablespoons (23 g) flour

2 cups (475 ml) warm chicken stock

4 ounces (114 g) hand-shredded Monterey Jack cheese

1 cup (230 g) sour cream

¼ cup (36 g) diced green or Hatch chiles

4 rolls (see bread recommendations)

4 ounces (114 g) hand-shredded Monterey Jack cheese

Diced green onions or cilantro for garnish

Pickled Red Onions (p. 183)

**BREAD RECOMMENDATIONS:**

Sesame hoagie rolls

Italian rolls

French baguette

Bolillo rolls

**Picking up a hot chicken enchilada just got a whole lot easier and way more fun. This toasty sandwich encourages you to get close and personal with smoked chicken coated in a spicy, cheesy sauce. Seriously, the crunch of the bread paired with that gooey cheese soaking in with every bite? It's delicious. Skip the flour tortillas and grab a sesame roll!**

**1.** Smoke the whole chicken as per the instructions on page 41. Once the meat is shredded, add in chili powder and the diced chiles. Keep the chicken warm while you prep the sandwich.

**2.** Next, make the sauce. Warm a saucepan over medium heat, add the butter, and whisk in the flour as to create a smooth roux. Slowly pour in the warm chicken stock, a little at a time, while whisking to keep the sauce smooth. Lower the heat, then gradually add half of the shredded cheese, whisking gently. Next, stir in the sour cream and fold in the diced chiles. Give it a good whisk, taste, and adjust the seasoning to make sure it's just right. Turn off the heat.

**3.** Preheat the broiler in the oven. Slice the bread lengthwise on the top and fill it with the shredded chicken. Ladle on some of the sauce and sprinkle with the remaining shredded cheese. Place the sandwich on a baking sheet lined with aluminum foil, then pop it under the broiler for 2 to 3 minutes—don't walk away, you don't want it to burn!

**4.** Once it's properly toasty, remove the baking sheet, top with garnishes of choice, and enjoy. Your first bite will be impossibly hot because you're likely as impatient as me. Don't say I didn't warn you.

# NASHVILLE HOT CHICKEN MELT

**MAKES 4 LARGE SANDWICHES**
**EQUIPMENT: SMOKER AND SKILLET**

**FOR NASHVILLE HOT SEASONING:**

- ⅓ cup (75 g) brown sugar
- ¼ cup (21 g) cayenne pepper powder
- 2 tablespoons (14 g) paprika
- 1 tablespoon (18 g) kosher salt
- 1 tablespoon (18 g) celery salt
- 2 teaspoons granulated garlic
- 2 teaspoons coarsely ground black pepper

- 2 cups (280 g) Smoked Pulled Chicken (p. 41)
- ¼ cup Nashville Hot Seasoning, plus more as needed
- Cayenne pepper powder, optional

**FOR NASHVILLE HOT MAYO:**

- 1 cup (225 g) Fresh Mayonnaise (p. 157)
- 3 tablespoons (44 ml) cayenne hot sauce, plus more as needed
- 1 teaspoon Nashville Hot Seasoning, plus more as needed

- 2 tablespoons (28 g) unsalted butter, divided
- 8 slices bread (see bread recommendations)
- 4 slices pepper jack cheese

**BREAD RECOMMENDATIONS:**

- Texas toast
- Pullman loaf
- Thin-sliced sourdough
- Potato bread

**It might have originated as a fried food, but trust me, Nashville hot chicken tastes amazing coming out of the smoker. I wanted to take some of my memories from Nashville and turn them into a simple, irresistible sandwich with all the classic elements: spicy, juicy chicken, crispy crust, and pillowy bread that soaks up all the flavors. Of course, pickles on the side. Add a layer of melty pepper jack cheese between crispy Texas toast, and you've got a literal flavor bomb that'll keep you up at night. Hopefully because you're dreaming about it, not dealing with indigestion.**

**1.** Make the Nashville Hot Seasoning by mixing all ingredients together in a small bowl.

**2.** Smoke the whole chicken as per the instructions on page 41 using the Nashville Hot Seasoning. Once the chicken is shredded, toss in some extra seasoning, taste, and adjust it to your heat level. If you're looking for more kick, add a little extra cayenne. Keep the chicken warm while you prep the sandwich.

**3.** For the spicy mayo, mix everything together and adjust with more hot sauce or seasoning if you like it extra fiery.

**4.** Preheat the oven to 200°F (93°C) and set up a baking sheet with a wire rack.

**CONTINUED →**

## NASHVILLE HOT CHICKEN MELT, CONTINUED

**5.** Heat a cast-iron skillet or griddle over medium-low heat, adding half of the unsalted butter. Spread the spicy mayo on each slice of bread. When the butter melts, place one slice of bread, mayo side down, in the skillet. Top with a slice of cheese, pile on the smoked chicken, another slice of cheese, and the second slice of bread, mayo side up. Once the underside is golden brown, after about 3 minutes, flip the sandwich and add the remaining butter. Press down gently to ensure even toasting and help the cheese melt.

**6.** Once the bread is perfectly browned, remove the sandwich and place it on the wire rack in the oven. Continue making the remaining sandwiches and let them rest in the oven for 3 to 5 minutes before serving. This step helps prevent soggy bread and ensures extra melty cheese.

**7.** Serve this sandwich with plenty of fresh pickles, chips, and a cold beverage of choice.

# PECAN CHICKEN SALAD

**MAKES 4 SANDWICHES**
**EQUIPMENT: SMOKER**

**FOR SMOKED PECANS:**

2 cups (220 g) pecans

1 tablespoon (15 ml) avocado oil

1 teaspoon kosher salt

1 teaspoon coarsely ground black pepper

1 tablespoon (15 g) brown sugar

1 teaspoon cayenne pepper

**FOR CHICKEN SALAD:**

4 cups (560 g) Smoked Pulled Chicken (p. 41)

2 ribs celery, diced

2 scallions, finely diced

1 cup (110 g) Smoked Pecans, chopped (recipe at right)

2 teaspoons Dijon mustard

⅔ cup (150 g) Fresh Mayonnaise (p. 157)

1 tablespoon (14 g) Sweet Smolder Rub (p. 173)

Juice of 1 lemon

2 hard-boiled eggs, peeled and diced

Salt and coarsely ground black pepper to taste

4 buns or rolls (see bread recommendations)

Softened butter, for toasting

Lettuce

**BREAD RECOMMENDATIONS:**

Poppy seed rolls

Kaiser rolls

Croissants

Potato buns

**Note:** Typically I'll smoke the pecans alongside the chicken to save time and fuel. It's always a good idea to fill up that smoker when you can!

**Smoked chicken salad is a game-changer, turning that boring shredded chicken into a flavor-packed dish. I like to smoke the chicken with pecan wood, which gives it a great bronze color and a mild, nutty flavor that pairs perfectly with the creamy dressing. Of course, it tastes even better with smoked pecans and crunchy veggies that add texture. Try adding chopped cranberries, golden raisins, diced apples, or even grapes**

**1.** Heat the smoker to 250°F (121°C). First, make the Smoked Pecans. Toss the pecans with the oil in a small bowl. Mix the salt, black pepper, brown sugar, and cayenne together and sprinkle them over the pecans, tossing again to coat evenly. Spread the pecans in a single layer on a baking sheet and smoke for 45 minutes, stirring halfway through. Remove and let them cool.

**2.** Shred the chicken into bite-sized pieces and add it to a large bowl along with the diced celery, scallions, pecans, Dijon, mayonnaise, rub, and lemon juice. Use a spatula to gently fold everything together. Add the diced eggs and fold them in carefully to avoid mashing them. Taste and adjust the seasoning as needed. Cover and refrigerate to allow the flavors to meld for at least an hour, or even overnight.

**3.** Toast a bun or croissant with a little butter in a pan, then pile on the chicken salad and top with your favorite leafy lettuce. This recipe is perfect for meal prep, school lunches, or even to serve guests with crackers at a party.

**Note:** For a smoother sauce, use an immersion blender to puree everything together. You can also transfer the contents to a blender, but be careful, as the sauce will be hot.

# SMOKED CREAMY CHICKEN

**MAKES 6 TO 8 SANDWICHES**
**EQUIPMENT: SMOKER AND DUTCH OVEN**

1¼ cups (296 ml) chicken stock
1 cup (235 ml) heavy cream
2 tablespoons (28 g) unsalted butter
1 sweet onion, diced
2 celery ribs, diced
3 garlic cloves, minced
2 tablespoons (15 g) all-purpose flour
2 teaspoons freshly ground black pepper, plus more to taste
1 teaspoon cayenne pepper
Kosher salt to taste
6 cups (840 g) Smoked Pulled Chicken (p. 41)

6 to 8 buns or rolls (see bread recommendations)
Softened butter, for toasting
Fresh Pickles (p. 178) or Quick Pickles (p. 181)

**BREAD RECOMMENDATIONS:**
Onion buns
Potato rolls
Brioche buns
Kaiser rolls

**Many nights when I was a kid, my mom would throw together some shredded chicken with a can of cream of gloop soup and serve it on buns or over rice. (Let's be real, I thought it was awesome.) This recipe recreates that nostalgic comfort, but with a simple twist—elevating it with homemade creamy gravy and smoked pulled chicken with a peppery kick. Make this, invite your mom over, and pay it back. And don't forget the pickles—they'll take the flavor up a notch and add the perfect zing.**

**1.** Warm the chicken stock and heavy cream in a small pot, keeping warm over low heat.

**2.** In a large pot, like a Dutch oven, melt the butter over medium heat. Add the onion and celery, cooking and stirring occasionally until softened and translucent, about 4 to 5 minutes. Add the garlic and cook until fragrant, about 1 minute. Sprinkle the flour over the vegetables and stir. Cook for 1 to 2 minutes until the flour is coating the veggies and no dry flour remains. Stir in black pepper and cayenne.

**3.** Gradually pour in the warm stock and cream mixture, a little at a time, whisking constantly. Bring to a boil, then reduce the heat to maintain a gentle simmer. Stir frequently and cook until the gravy thickens just enough to coat the back of a spoon, about 7 to 8 minutes. Taste and adjust the seasoning with salt and pepper as needed.

**4.** Add the shredded chicken to the sauce and stir to heat through. Let it simmer for about 5 minutes before serving.

**5.** Top your choice of toasted buns or rolls with plenty of creamy chicken and crispy pickles. This is all you need!

3

# LET IT ROLL: MODERATE EFFORT, BIG FLAVOR

# BLUE CHEESE AND BACON JAM BURGER

**MAKES 4 BURGERS**
**EQUIPMENT: CHARCOAL GRILL AND SKILLET**

**FOR BACON JAM:**

1 pound (454 g) bacon, diced

1 tablespoon (14 g) unsalted butter

2 sweet onions, diced

¼ cup (60 g) dark brown sugar

¼ cup (59 ml) apple cider vinegar

2 tablespoons (30 ml) balsamic vinegar

1 tablespoon (9 g) minced chipotles in adobo

2 tablespoons (40 g) honey

½ cup (118 ml) water

½ teaspoon freshly ground black pepper

1½ pounds (680 g) ground beef, 80/20 preferred

Kosher salt and freshly ground black pepper to taste

Soft blue cheese, such as Roquefort or Cambozola

Softened butter, for toasting

8 burger buns (see bread recommendations)

Sour Cream Sandwich Sauce (p. 159)

Green apples, sliced

Arugula, optional

**BREAD RECOMMENDATIONS:**

Brioche buns

Potato rolls

Kaiser rolls

Onion buns

**Sometimes, you need a burger that has it all. Charcoal-kissed with accents of salty, rich, tangy, and smoky, this burger has the perfect balance of flavors. The bacon jam brings a sweet and savory punch along with crispy bacon and caramelized onions, but I wanted to make sure it didn't steal the show. Crisp apples paired with blue cheese and a hint of balsamic tie everything together, cutting through the richness with a bit of cream and crunch. If you need some leafy greens, arugula works well, otherwise this fully loaded burger is already so stacked that it might need its own zip code.**

**1.** Start by preparing the bacon jam, as this will take the longest to cook and can be made ahead of time. Heat a large skillet over medium heat. Add the bacon and cook until crispy. Using a slotted spoon, transfer the cooked bacon to a paper towel–lined plate. Drain most of the bacon grease, leaving about 2 tablespoons (30 ml) in the skillet.

**2.** Add the butter and onions to the skillet. Stir to coat the onions with the fat and cook over low heat, covering the onions with a circle of parchment paper to prevent them from drying out. Cook for about 10 minutes, lifting the paper and stirring occasionally as the onions begin to brown. Continue cooking over low heat for another 10 to 15 minutes, until the onions are caramelized.

**3.** Add the brown sugar, cider vinegar, balsamic vinegar, chipotles, honey, water, and black pepper. Return the cooked bacon to the pan. Bring the mixture to a boil, then lower the heat and simmer for about 20 minutes, until the liquid reduces and the consistency becomes thick and syrupy. Remove from the heat—the bacon jam will continue to thicken as it cools. Store it in the fridge, where it will stay fresh for at least a week. When ready to use, warm it up slowly in a pan.

**CONTINUED** →

## BLUE CHEESE AND BACON JAM BURGER, CONTINUED

**4.** Gently form the ground beef into 4 patties, about ½-inch (1 cm) wider than the burger buns, with a slight press in the center to prevent bulging. Season generously with salt and pepper.

**5.** Preheat the grill for two-zone cooking by banking the coals to one side, aiming for a temperature around 400°F (204°C). Clean the grilling grates, then gently place the burgers directly over the hot coals.

**6.** Allow the burgers to cook for about 3 to 4 minutes, flipping when they have visible grill marks and release easily from the grates. Spoon on some of the blue cheese and continue cooking for another 3 to 4 minutes, or until they're nearly at your preferred doneness. Move the burgers to the cool side of the grill to rest.

**7.** Place the buttered buns on the grill grates and toast them briefly while the coals are still hot. Once everything's off the grill, it's time to assemble the burgers.

**8.** Start with the toasted bun, a dollop of the sandwich sauce, a grilled burger with blue cheese, thin slices of apple, a generous portion of the warmed bacon jam, and arugula if using. Top with the toasted bun, and you've got a complete meal—dripping down and ready for you to dig into.

# SMOKED BRAT BURGERS

**MAKES 4 BURGERS**
**EQUIPMENT: CHARCOAL GRILL OR SMOKER**

6 uncooked bratwurst, about 20 to 24 ounces (567 to 680 g)

Fresh ground pepper, to taste

**FOR HORSERADISH DIJONNAISE:**

½ cup (115 g) Fresh Mayonnaise (p. 157)

2 tablespoons (22 g) Dijon mustard

1 tablespoon (15 g) prepared horseradish

1 teaspoon fresh dill, chopped

1 teaspoon pickle juice

Salt to taste

4 slices Butterkäse, Havarti, or Muenster cheese

Softened butter, for toasting

4 buns (see bread recommendations)

Pickled Brussels sprouts (p. 184) or sauerkraut

Fresh Pickles (p. 178) or Quick Pickles (p. 181), optional

**BREAD RECOMMENDATIONS:**

Onion buns

Pretzel buns

Kaiser rolls

Poppy seed buns

**Classic bratwurst flavors meet the burger bun, creating a savory, crispy burger packed with juicy, meaty goodness. The meat is removed from the casing, formed into patties, and slowly smoked and seared to bring out a new layer of flavor, all while preserving that authentic bratwurst taste. These burgers are ready for whatever toppings you love on your German sausages. My go-to? Spicy Dijonnaise, melty cheese, and a pile of pickled Brussels sprouts or sauerkraut. One bite, and you'll agree, this is the wurst burger.**

**1.** Take a sharp knife and run it down the bratwurst casings to remove the meat. Form the meat into 4 burger patties, about ½-inch (1-cm) thick, and press a small indent in the center to prevent them from puffing up during cooking. Season generously with black pepper, then place the patties on a parchment paper–lined baking sheet. Chill them in the fridge for about 20 minutes to reinforce their shape.

**2.** While the patties are chilling, mix up the Horseradish Dijonnaise by combining all the ingredients. Season to taste, then let it chill in the fridge until it's time to top those burgers.

**3.** Preheat the smoker or grill for indirect cooking. A charcoal grill works great for this, especially because you'll be searing the burgers at the end. Set up your grill with a hot side for searing and a cool side for smoking, aiming for an internal temperature of about 275°F to 300°F (135°C to 149°C). Add wood chips or chunks to the coals to give some extra flavor.

**CONTINUED →**

## SMOKED BRAT BURGERS, CONTINUED

**4.** Place the brat burgers on the cool side of the grill, away from the coals, and smoke them with the lid closed for 30 to 40 minutes until they reach 145°F to 150°F (63°C to 66°C) internal temperature. Once they hit that target, move them over the coals and sear for 2 to 3 minutes per side until they're nicely browned and done. Keep an eye on those flare-ups from the pork fat—they'll sneak up on you! Add slices of cheese to the burgers and let them melt for about a minute. Remove the burgers from the grill when they reach an internal temperature of 155°F to 160°F (66°C to 71°C).

**5.** While the burgers are resting, toast the buttered buns on the grill for just a minute, until golden brown.

**6.** Now, assemble the sandwiches. Spread a little sauce on the bottom bun, top with some Brussels sprouts or sauerkraut, add the cheeseburger, and finish with the top bun. For an extra kick, top with homemade pickles.

**7.** Serve these burgers with pretzels and a cold beer for the ultimate bratwurst experience.

# SMOKED CHOPPED CHEESE

**MAKES 4 SANDWICHES**
**EQUIPMENT: SMOKER AND GRIDDLE**

1 tomato, sliced thin
Kosher salt as needed
1¼ pounds (20 ounces) (567 g) ground beef, 85/15
2 tablespoons (26 g) Prime Smoke Rub (p. 173)
1 tablespoon (14 g) unsalted butter
1 small onion, diced
2 tablespoons (18 g) chipotles in adobo, minced
8 slices American cheese
4 hoagie rolls (see bread recommendations)
¼ cup (60 g) Fresh Mayonnaise (p. 157)
3 tablespoons (44 ml) House BBQ Sauce (p. 163)
1 cup (55 g) lettuce, thinly sliced
Fresh Pickles (p. 178) or Quick Pickles (p. 181)

**BREAD RECOMMENDATIONS:**
Italian hoagie rolls
French rolls
Baguette
Bolillo rolls

**Pro Tip:** The louder you chop, the better it tastes (so I'm told).

**It's hard to mess with a classic, but I don't play by the rules. Slowly smoking the beef before searing adds an extra layer of flavor and dries out the surface for more crust development when seared. Smoky, crispy, and loaded with texture, this sandwich has it all. Plus, there's still plenty of melty cheese and a few fresh toppings to brighten it up. Throw in some pickle slices and watch the New Yorkers lose their minds.**

**1.** Preheat the smoker to 225°F (107°C). This recipe works best with a pellet smoker, but you can also use a two-zone setup on a charcoal grill.

**2.** Salt the tomato slices lightly on both sides and press them between paper towels, letting them sit for at least 10 minutes to drain off some of the liquid.

**3.** Divide the beef into 4 large portions, pressing just enough to hold their shape. Dust the beef with seasoning on all sides, then place the portions in the smoker. Let the beef cook for 30 to 35 minutes until the outside develops a brick-red tone. Remove the beef and get ready to sear.

**4.** Heat a griddle or cast-iron skillet over medium-high heat. Melt the butter, then add the diced onions. Cook for a few minutes until they start to soften, then push them to the side. Add the smoked beef portions to the skillet, pressing them down to sear and develop a nice crust. Flip the beef and sear the other side. Once the beef is seared, add the minced chipotles and chop everything together with the onions, mixing well.

**5.** Lower the heat of the griddle or stovetop. Spread the meat out into even portions and add the American cheese slices on top. Once melted, chop the cheese in with the meat and get ready to assemble the sandwiches.

**6.** Open up the rolls and slather some of the mayonnaise and BBQ sauce on the inside. Stack layers of sliced tomatoes, chopped lettuce, pickles (if that's your thing), and cheesy beef. Immediately roll up the sandwich in foil or parchment paper and allow it to rest for a minute—this lets the flavors mingle and keeps it from falling apart. Rip it open and chow down!

# ENCHILADA BURGER

**MAKES 4 BURGERS**
**EQUIPMENT: CHARCOAL GRILL AND SKILLET**

**FOR ENCHILADA SAUCE:**

10 dried guajillo chiles, stemmed, seeded, and torn into large pieces

4 garlic cloves, peeled and roughly chopped

15 ounces (525 g) diced fire-roasted tomatoes, with juices

½ cup (118 ml) water

2 tablespoons (30 ml) avocado oil

3 cups (710 ml) chicken broth

Pinch white sugar

Salt to taste

1½ pounds (680 g) ground beef, 80/20 preferred

Kosher salt and freshly ground black pepper

4 slices Monterey Jack or pepper jack cheese

Softened butter, for toasting

4 buns (see bread recommendations)

Pickled Jalapeños (p. 182)

Pickled Red Onions (p. 183)

½ head red cabbage, finely shredded on a mandolin or by hand

1 tablespoon (18 g) kosher salt

Mexican crema

Cotija cheese

**BREAD RECOMMENDATIONS:**

Sesame seed buns

Torta rolls

Potato rolls

Conchas

Enchiladas have come a long way, moving beyond the cheese-smothered casserole and into a world of fresh, vibrant toppings that bring balance to every bite. This charcoal-grilled burger, cooked over mesquite, brings that carne asada flavor straight to the bun, topped with a spicy red sauce and piled high with crispy, tangy goodness. It's like your favorite enchilada, but without the fork. Just don't wear white, and make sure you've got extra napkins nearby.

**1.** Prepare the enchilada sauce, which can be made ahead of time. Heat a dry cast-iron skillet over medium heat and toast the chiles for about 30 seconds per side. Transfer the chiles to a bowl and cover them with hot (but not boiling) water to rehydrate. Cover the bowl with a towel and let them sit for about 20 minutes.

**2.** Once the chiles are rehydrated, remove them with tongs and transfer them to a blender or food processor. Add the garlic, tomatoes with their juices, and water, then blend to a smooth puree. Strain the sauce through a sieve into a bowl.

**CONTINUED** →

## ENCHILADA BURGER, CONTINUED

**3.** Heat a Dutch oven or deep skillet over medium-high heat—make sure the pot has a lid. Add the oil to coat. Add the chile sauce and stir frequently, cooking for about 5 minutes until it begins to thicken. Add the chicken broth, partially cover the pot, and simmer over medium-low heat for about 15 to 20 minutes. Taste and season with sugar and salt as needed. Remove from the heat.

**4.** Gently form the ground beef into 4 patties, about ½-inch (1-cm) wider than the burger buns, with a slight press in the center to prevent bulging. Season generously with salt and pepper.

**5.** Preheat the grill for two-zone cooking by banking the coals to one side, aiming for a temperature around 400°F (204°C). Add chunks of mesquite hardwood or wood chips. Once the wood has smoldered, clean the grilling grates, then gently place the burgers directly over the hot coals.

**6.** Allow the burgers to cook for about 3 to 4 minutes, flipping when they have visible grill marks and release easily from the grates. Add a slice of cheese and continue to cook for another 3 to 4 minutes, or until they're nearly at your preferred doneness. Move the burgers to the cool side of the grill to rest.

**7.** Place the buttered buns on the grill grates and toast them briefly while the coals are still hot. Once everything's off the grill, it's time to assemble the burgers.

**8.** Start with the toasted bun, a grilled cheeseburger, a healthy drizzle of the sauce, pickled jalapeños and onions, cabbage, crema, and cotija cheese.

# KOREAN STOUT PULLED BEEF

**MAKES 8 TO 10 SANDWICHES**
**EQUIPMENT: SMOKER**

**FOR KIMCHI SLAW:**

½ small napa cabbage, shredded, about 4 cups (280 g)

4 scallions, julienned lengthwise

4 radishes, shaved and quartered

1 cup (142 g) kimchi, drained and chopped

1 garlic clove, grated

⅓ cup (75 g) Kewpie mayo or Fresh Mayonnaise (p. 157)

1 tablespoon (11 g) Dijon mustard

Juice of 1 lemon

2 tablespoons (30 g) gochugaru (Korean chili flakes), optional for heat

Salt to taste

⅓ cup (67 g) Prime Smoke Rub (p. 173)

1 chuck roast, about 3 to 4 pounds (1.4 to 1.8 kg)

**FOR KOREAN STOUT BBQ SAUCE:**

1 bottle (12 ounces [355ml]) dark stout beer

½ cup (115 g) brown sugar

¼ cup (80 g) maple syrup

¼ cup (59 ml) soy sauce

½ cup (120 g) ketchup

3 tablespoons (45 g) gochujang (Korean chili paste)

1 tablespoon (15 ml) Worcestershire sauce

1 teaspoon onion powder

1 teaspoon garlic powder

½ sweet onion, sliced thin

1 cup (235 ml) beef broth

8 to 10 buns or rolls (see bread recommendations)

Softened butter, for toasting

Fresh Pickles (p. 178) or Quick Pickles (p. 181)

**BREAD RECOMMENDATIONS:**

Brioche buns

Sesame buns

Portuguese rolls

Potato buns

**This sandwich will have you loosening your belt and reaching for another beer. We're talking slow-smoked chuck roast braised and shredded to perfection, drenched in a spicy stout sauce that ignites your taste buds. The crunchy kimchi slaw cuts through the richness of the beef, balancing everything out for the perfect bite. It's juicy, savory, and packs just the right amount of heat.**

**1.** Prepare the Kimchi Slaw ahead of time if possible. Add all the ingredients to a large bowl and mix well, making sure the veggies are fully coated in the dressing. Taste and adjust with salt or chili flakes for more heat. Cover and store in the fridge until ready to use—it's even better if the flavors have a few hours to meld together before serving.

**2.** Preheat the smoker to 250°F (121°C). Season the chuck roast generously on all sides and let it rest at room temperature while the smoker warms up. Place the beef in the smoker and cook for about 3 hours, or until it reaches an internal temperature of around 165°F (74°C).

CONTINUED →

## KOREAN STOUT PULLED BEEF, CONTINUED

**3.** While the beef is smoking, make the stout BBQ sauce. In a saucepan, add the beer and bring it to a boil. Once boiling, reduce the heat slightly and let it simmer for 8 to 10 minutes to reduce the liquid, concentrate the flavor, and cook off the alcohol. Lower the heat to medium-low and whisk in the rest of the ingredients. Let it simmer on low for 6 to 8 minutes, or until it thickens up just enough. Turn off the heat and set aside.

**4.** Check the chuck roast. Once it reaches the target temperature, add it to a foil pan with the sliced onions and beef broth. Wrap the top tightly with heavy-duty foil, add the pan back to the smoker, and increase the heat to 275°F (135°C). Cook for an hour, then open the foil pan and flip the beef. Cover it again and continue to cook for another 1 to 2 hours, or until the meat reaches around 205°F (96°C) and is probe-tender. Timing may vary depending on the size of the chuck roast and its fat marbling. Once it's done, remove the pan and let the beef rest, covered, for 30 to 45 minutes, or until it's cool enough to handle.

**5.** Shred the meat, discarding any unwanted fat, and mix in 1 cup (235 ml) BBQ sauce. Pile the mixture onto buttered and toasted buns with more sauce, the slaw, and some pickles. Hopefully, you still have some beer left to enjoy with it, because it pairs perfectly.

# UMAMI BOMB

**MAKES 4 BURGERS**
**EQUIPMENT: CHARCOAL GRILL AND SKILLET**

**FOR THE MUSHROOMS:**

4 large portobello mushrooms

3 tablespoons (44 ml) balsamic vinegar

2 tablespoons (30 ml) soy sauce

1 tablespoon (15 ml) olive oil

1 tablespoon (6 g) coarsely ground black pepper

2 teaspoons garlic powder

1 teaspoon cayenne pepper

1½ pounds (680 g) ground beef, 80/20 preferred

Kosher salt and freshly ground black pepper to taste

4 slices Havarti cheese

1 red onion, sliced into thick rings

Black Garlic Mayo (p. 158)

4 burger buns (see bread recommendations)

Tomato, sliced

**BREAD RECOMMENDATIONS:**

Sesame seed buns

Telera rolls

Kaiser rolls

Onion buns

**I love experimenting with layers of flavor. Umami is one of the most exciting (yet underused, besides bacon, of course) taste profiles in barbecue. When it comes to this burger, it's hard to pick a star. The marinated mushrooms, fresh slices of tomato, and that deep, rich black garlic mayo each bring their own mouth-watering punch of flavor. Don't forget the seared beef; that's the heart of this burger. Every bite is a flavor bomb, and trust me, it's impossible to put down.**

**1.** Prepare the mushrooms first so they have time to marinate. Prepare the portobellos by removing the stems and gills and wiping the caps clean. Then toss them into a large resealable bag. In a small bowl, combine the other ingredients and whisk together. Pour the marinade over the mushrooms, gently mix everything around, and remove as much air from the bag as you can before sealing. Let them marinate for at least 30 to 60 minutes while you get the grill ready.

**2.** Form the ground beef into individual patties, being careful not to overwork the meat. Press a small indentation in the center to keep them from swelling up as they cook. Season both sides generously with salt and pepper.

**3.** Preheat the grill for two-zone cooking, banking the coals to one side to reach around 400°F (204°C). Place the burgers on the grill, but don't press down—let them sear for 3 to 4 minutes before flipping. After both sides are seared, move the burgers to the cooler side of the grill, top with the cheese, and let them finish cooking while you get the mushrooms going.

**CONTINUED →**

## UMAMI BOMB, CONTINUED

**4.** Grill the red onion slices, charring them on both sides until they're nice and caramelized. Shake off any excess marinade from the mushrooms and reserve it for basting. Place the mushrooms on the grill and cook them for 3 to 4 minutes per side, basting them with the reserved marinade as they cook. They should end up caramelized and a deep golden brown.

**5.** Check the temperature of the burgers to make sure they're cooked to your preferred doneness, then remove everything from the grill. Toast the burger buns with a little of the Black Garlic Mayonnaise on the grill while you finish up.

**6.** Assemble the burger by spreading some more garlic mayo on the bottom bun, followed by slices of fresh tomato, the cheesy burger, grilled mushroom, and caramelized red onions. Top with more black garlic mayo and a grind of freshly cracked black pepper. Place the top bun on, and get ready to enjoy one of the most savory burgers you've ever sunk your teeth into.

# SMOKED SALMON BAGEL

**MAKES 4 SANDWICHES**
**EQUIPMENT: SMOKER**

3 cups (710 ml) cold water

¼ cup (75 g) kosher salt

4 salmon fillets with skin, 4 to 5 ounces each (113 to 142 g)

Freshly ground black pepper

**FOR CUCUMBER SALAD:**

1 large English cucumber, very thinly sliced

½ shallot, very thinly sliced

⅓ cup (79 ml) rice vinegar

1 tablespoon (8 g) sesame seeds, toasted

1 tablespoon (4 g) minced dill

¾ teaspoon salt

¾ teaspoon sugar

¼ teaspoon red pepper flakes, crushed

**FOR JALAPEÑO CREAM CHEESE:**

1 jalapeño, finely diced

8 ounces (227 g) cream cheese

1 tablespoon (9 g) garlic powder

1 teaspoon onion powder

Salt to taste

3 scallions

Softened butter, for toasting

4 bagels, sliced (see bread recommendations)

Lemon juice

Dill, minced for garnish

Lemon wedges

**BREAD RECOMMENDATIONS:**

Everything bagels

Ciabatta

Focaccia

Kaiser rolls

I'll be honest, this smoked salmon bagel started as a "what do I have in the fridge?" kind of moment and turned into something I make regularly. It's simple: brine the salmon, let the smoker do its thing, and top it all off with a tangy cucumber salad and a spicy cream cheese. Pile it all onto a heavily seasoned bagel, and you've got yourself a dang tasty sandwich. Whether you're prepping for breakfast or craving something lighter at dinner, this one's got all the flavor you need. You won't miss the bacon for a second.

**1.** Start by preparing the brine. In a bowl, combine water and salt, stirring until the salt is fully dissolved. Place the salmon fillets in a small casserole dish and pour the brine over the fish, ensuring it's fully covered. If you need more liquid, repeat the process. Cover the dish and refrigerate for 2 hours.

**2.** After brining, remove the salmon from the liquid and pat dry with paper towels. Season with black pepper, then transfer the fish to a baking sheet. Place the baking sheet in the fridge for 2 to 4 hours to allow the fish to form a pellicle—a dry, tacky layer that helps the salmon absorb the smoke flavor.

CONTINUED →

## SMOKED SALMON BAGEL, CONTINUED

**3.** Prepare the Cucumber Salad while the salmon chills. In a medium bowl, mix all the ingredients and gently toss to coat the cucumbers. Let it sit in the fridge for a few hours so the flavors can really come together.

**4.** For the Jalapeño Cream Cheese, combine the ingredients and give it a taste. Adjust seasoning as needed. This will stay fresh in the fridge for 3 to 5 days.

**5.** When you're ready to smoke the salmon, remove it from the fridge. Preheat your pellet grill or charcoal grill with a two-zone setup to a low 230°F (110°C). Place the salmon fillets on the grill, skin-side down, and smoke until they reach your preferred doneness—usually between 125°F to 135°F (52°C to 57°C), which should take about 30 to 45 minutes depending on the size of the fillets.

**6.** Once the salmon is ready, remove it from the grill and crank the heat up to 350°F (177°C). If you're using a charcoal grill, take off the lid and let the hot coals do their thing. Toss the scallions on the grill for a few minutes until they get a slight char, then remove them. Next, butter your bagels and toast them on the grill until golden brown.

**7.** Trim the ends of the scallions and mince them up finely. Season with a little lemon juice for extra freshness. To assemble the sandwiches, spread some Jalapeño Cream Cheese on the bagel, add a layer of Cucumber Salad, then follow with the smoked salmon and charred scallions. Serve with a sprinkle of extra dill and lemon wedges on the side.

# SMOKED MEATLOAF PATTY MELT

**MAKES 8 TO 10 SANDWICHES**
**EQUIPMENT: SMOKER AND SKILLET**

¾ cup (38 g) panko breadcrumbs

2 eggs, whisked

½ cup (118 ml) non-skim milk

1½ tablespoons (22 ml) Worcestershire sauce

2 teaspoons garlic powder

1 tablespoon (4 g) chopped fresh parsley

2 teaspoons chopped fresh thyme

2 tablespoons (22 g) Dijon mustard

2 pounds (907 g) ground beef, 80/20 preferred

2 teaspoons kosher salt, plus more as needed

1 teaspoon coarsely ground black pepper, plus more as needed

Avocado oil

4 sweet onions, sliced thin on a mandolin or by hand

Kosher salt

2 tablespoons (28 g) unsalted butter, plus more as needed

Water, as needed

16 to 20 slices bread (see bread recommendations)

Spicy Dijonnaise (p. 37, Smoked Pastrami Steak)

16 to 20 slices Gruyère or Swiss cheese

**BREAD RECOMMENDATIONS:**

Jewish rye bread

Caraway rye bread

Thin-sliced sourdough

Pumpernickel bread

**I grew up with the classic Midwest oven-baked meatloaf glazed with ketchup. I didn't realize how much I could actually love meatloaf until I had a unique meatloaf sandwich at a brewery in my twenties. The juicy slice of seasoned beef, melty cheese, buttery onions, and juices all soaked up in toasty bread create a savory bite that makes you forget all about those ketchup days. Dig into this caramelized onion goodness that hopefully revives your love for meatloaf, just like it did for me.**

**1.** Place the breadcrumbs in a large bowl. Add the whisked eggs, milk, Worcestershire sauce, garlic powder, parsley, thyme, and Dijon mustard. Using a fork, gently mix all the ingredients together, then let it sit for about 5 minutes to soak up everything. This is the panada, which will evenly season the meatloaf while keeping it moist and tender.

**2.** Add the ground beef, salt, and pepper. Gently mix with your hands to incorporate the panada without overworking the meat. Once thoroughly mixed, heat a small pan over medium-high heat with a drop of oil. Form a small beef patty and brown both sides until it's cooked through to test the flavor. Adjust with more salt or seasoning if needed.

**CONTINUED →**

## SMOKED MEATLOAF PATTY MELT, CONTINUED

**3.** Line a baking sheet with parchment paper. Place the meat mixture into the center of the sheet and form a loaf shape, making sure it's at least as wide as the bread you'll be using. Set the pan in the fridge and allow the meatloaf to chill for 30 minutes, which helps it hold its shape and absorb all of the flavors.

**4.** Start cooking the onions, as they'll take a bit of time. Use a wide skillet or nonstick pan and warm it over medium-low heat. Add the sliced onions and sprinkle lightly with salt, stirring to coat. Cook for 30 to 40 minutes, stirring occasionally as the onions begin to brown. Add the butter and continue to cook, stirring as needed, until they reach your desired level of caramelization. Be sure to taste along the way.

**5.** Preheat the smoker to 350°F (177°C) while the onions are cooking. If grilling, set up a two-zone cooking method by banking the coals to one side. Place the baking sheet with the meatloaf into the smoker and let it cook for 45 to 50 minutes undisturbed. The target internal temperature is 160°F (71°C). Once it hits that mark, take the pan out and let the meatloaf rest for at least 10 to 15 minutes. Slice the meatloaf.

**6.** Remove the onions from the pan and set them aside—you can use the same buttered pan for toasting the sandwich. Warm the pan over medium-low heat, adding a small knob of unsalted butter. Spread the Dijonnaise on each slice of bread. Once the butter melts, place one slice of bread, sauce-side up, in the skillet. Top with a slice of cheese, caramelized onions, two slices of meatloaf, more onions, another slice of cheese, and the second slice of bread, sauce-side down.

**7.** Cook until the underside is golden brown, about 3 minutes, then flip the sandwich and add more butter. Press down gently to ensure even toasting and help the cheese melt.

**8.** Once the bread is perfectly browned, remove the sandwich. You can keep it warm in the oven at a low temperature on a wire rack while you prepare the rest, which helps prevent soggy bread and ensures extra melty cheese.

**Note:** The slow-cooking and early addition of salt will help release the water from the onions, allowing them to brown without extra oil. If they stick to the pan, add a tiny splash of water to loosen them up. However, stirring occasionally should help prevent sticking.

# MAHI MAHI AL PASTOR

**MAKES 4 SANDWICHES**
**EQUIPMENT: CHARCOAL GRILL**

- ¼ cup (60 g) achiote paste
- ½ cup (118 ml) orange juice
- ½ cup (118 ml) juice from 1 can (20 ounces [567 g]) pineapple slices, slices reserved for relish
- 1 teaspoon dried Mexican oregano
- 1 garlic clove, grated
- ½ teaspoon kosher salt
- ¼ teaspoon freshly ground black pepper
- 4 mahi mahi fish fillets, 4 ounces (113 g) each
- 1 tablespoon (15 ml) avocado oil, plus more as needed

**FOR PINEAPPLE JALAPEÑO RELISH:**

- 1 can (20 ounces [567 g]) pineapple slices, juice reserved for marinade
- 2 jalapeños
- 1 tablespoon (15 ml) avocado oil
- Kosher salt and coarsely ground black pepper

- 4 rolls (see bread recommendations)
- Softened butter, for toasting
- Chipotle Mayonnaise (p. 158)
- Crispy Sandwich Slaw (p. 167)
- Pickled Red Onions (p. 183)

**BREAD RECOMMENDATIONS:**

- Telera rolls
- Torta bread
- Bolillo rolls
- Kaiser rolls
- Potato rolls

This bold marinade of chiles and citrus is perfect for fish, so I had to turn it into a sandwich. Al pastor is typically made with slow-roasted pork stacked high on a *trompo* spit. Instead, we're using that vibrant red marinade on mild, meaty mahi mahi, letting the fish soak up all that flavor before it hits the grill. The result? A smoky, tangy fish paired with fire-roasted pineapple jalapeño relish, crispy slaw, and tangy pickled red onions. It's fresh, spicy, and works perfectly on a toasted soft roll. Forget the tortillas. Stack on the toppings and dig in!

**1.** Prepare the marinade by combining the achiote paste, orange juice, pineapple juice (from the can of pineapple slices), oregano, garlic, salt, and pepper in a medium bowl. Mix everything together, then add the fish fillets, tossing to coat. Cover with plastic wrap and let it marinate in the fridge for 1 to 2 hours.

**2.** Preheat the grill for two-zone cooking by banking the coals to one side, aiming for a temperature around 400°F (204°C).

CONTINUED →

## MAHI MAHI AL PASTOR, CONTINUED

**3.** Pat the pineapple slices dry with paper towels. Brush the jalapeños and pineapple slices lightly with oil, then place them on the grill grates. Char them over the coals for a few minutes until grill marks appear, then remove. If you prefer less heat, remove the seeds from the jalapeños; otherwise, just slice off the stems. Add both the jalapeños and pineapple slices to a food processor and blend until smooth. Season with salt and pepper to taste, then set aside.

**4.** Clean the grill grates before adding the fish. Wipe off the excess marinade from the fillets and lightly brush them with oil. Sear the fish over the coals for 2 to 3 minutes per side, until grill marks form. Once both sides are marked, move the fish to the cooler side of the grill, close the lid, and let it cook for a few more minutes, or until it reaches an internal temperature of about 130°F (54°C). Remove the fish from the grill and let it rest.

**5.** If toasting the rolls, spread a little softened butter or Chipotle Mayonnaise on and toast on the grill for about a minute, or until light grill marks appear.

**6.** Assemble the sandwich with Chipotle Mayonnaise on the bottom bun, a little Crispy Sandwich Slaw, the grilled fish, some Pineapple Jalapeño Relish, and Pickled Red Onions. Top with more of the mayo and dig in. Enjoy this sandwich while wearing a pair of sunglasses for maximum pleasure.

# SMOKED TURKEY BREAST

**SERVES ABOUT 8 TO 10**
**EQUIPMENT: SMOKER**

---

- 1 boneless turkey breast, about 4 to 5 pounds (1.8 to 2.3 kg)
- ¼ cup (56 g) Sweet Smolder Rub (p. 174), plus more as needed
- ¼ cup (56 g) unsalted butter, divided into 4 pats

**Smoking your own deli meat at home makes all the difference for sandwiches. Whenever I find a good turkey breast at the butcher, you can bet it's heading straight for the smoker. This recipe makes a slightly sweet, peppery crust on the outside, perfect for piling up slices to make some of the best sandwiches. You don't need to get too fancy with the toppings—just enjoy that amazing smoked turkey.**

**1.** Start by prepping the turkey breast—use a sharp knife to remove the skin, then pat it dry with paper towels. Generously season the turkey on all sides with the rub. Let the turkey rest at room temperature while your smoker heats up to 250°F (121°C). If you're prepping ahead, place the turkey on a baking sheet in the fridge, uncovered, and let it rest overnight.

**2.** Once the smoker is ready, place the turkey in and let it cook for about 90 to 120 minutes, or until it reaches 145°F (63°C). Lay out a large sheet of heavy-duty foil and place the butter in the center. When the turkey hits the target temp, remove it from the smoker and set it on top of the butter (ugly side down). Wrap it tightly, making sure the ugly side is facing up when it goes back into the smoker. Continue smoking for another 30 to 40 minutes until the turkey reaches 158°F to 160°F (70°C to 71°C).

**3.** Remove the turkey from the smoker and let it rest, still wrapped, for at least 30 minutes before slicing. Don't slice it until you're ready to serve—it'll stay much juicier that way. Slice against the grain for tender bites, which runs along the length of the turkey breast, almost like you're carving a Thanksgiving bird.

**Note:** Cook and resting time will vary depending on the size of the turkey breast, so focus on the internal temperature more than anything.

# SMOKEHOUSE TURKEY CLUB

**MAKES 4 SANDWICHES**
**EQUIPMENT: SKILLET OR GRIDDLE**

---

**FOR ALABAMA WHITE SANDWICH SAUCE:**

1½ cups (340 g) Fresh Mayonnaise (p. 157)

¼ cup (59 ml) apple cider vinegar

Juice of 1 lemon

1 teaspoon hot sauce

½ teaspoon Worcestershire sauce

½ teaspoon garlic powder

½ teaspoon onion powder

½ teaspoon freshly ground black pepper

Salt to taste

Softened butter, for toasting

8 slices bread (see bread recommendations)

12 slices thick-cut bacon, cooked per instructions, plus more as needed

1½ pounds (680 g) Smoked Turkey Breast (p. 78), sliced thin

Tomatoes, sliced

Lettuce leaves

**BREAD RECOMMENDATIONS:**

Thin-sliced sourdough

Levain bread

Pullman loaf

Jewish rye bread

**The classic club sandwich is pretty unbeatable, but smoke the turkey yourself and you've figured out how to level up. Imagine thick slices of wood-fired turkey paired with all the classic toppings: lettuce, tomato, and crispy bacon. I find that smoked turkey needs a little zing, so this sandwich has an appropriately thick Alabama White Sandwich Sauce to bring it all home. Smoke the turkey breast in advance, and you'll have everything you need for a killer sandwich, whether it's a quick snack or a feast for the crew.**

**1.** In a small bowl, mix the ingredients for the sandwich sauce and set in the fridge until ready. Heat a griddle or heavy skillet over medium heat. Butter the bread and lightly toast the slices to golden perfection. Cook the bacon until it's crispy, or however you like it—at least 3 slices per sandwich is recommended (I'll never put a limit).

**2.** Now, assemble the sandwich: Start with a slice of bread, spread some sauce, and add lettuce, tomato, turkey, and bacon. Top with another slice of bread, then repeat with more sauce, lettuce, tomato, turkey, and bacon. Finish with the final slice of bread. Give it a solid press before you dive in, unless you're ready for a monster bite!

# POOL PARTY SANDWICH

**MAKES 4 SANDWICHES**
**EQUIPMENT: SKILLET OR GRIDDLE**

---

- 8 slices bread (see bread recommendations)
- Softened butter, for toasting
- ¼ cup (60 g) Chipotle Mayonnaise (p. 158)
- 1 cup (55 g) shredded lettuce
- 1½ pounds (680 g) Smoked Turkey Breast (p. 78), sliced thin
- 4 thick slices sharp cheddar cheese
- Potato chips

**BREAD RECOMMENDATIONS:**

- Texas toast
- White bread
- Pullman loaf
- Levain bread
- Wheat bread

**Nothing says "childhood sandwich" like the deli sandwich my mom would have ready when I crawled out of the pool on a scorching summer day. Plain, untoasted bread with mayo, a mountain of cold deli meat, and a little shredded lettuce tucked in (for fiber, of course). My chlorinated hands would grab a handful of potato chips to stack in the sandwich, and I'd scarf it down as fast as I could to get back in the pool. Now I'm a bit bigger and hungrier, so instead of the quick deli sandwich, I'm going all in with homemade smoked turkey on Texas toast, slathered in spicy chipotle mayo and ruffled chips.**

**1.** Toast the bread by heating a griddle or heavy skillet over medium heat. Butter the bread and toast each side for about 2 to 3 minutes, until golden and crisp.

**2.** Spread some Chipotle Mayonnaise on the toasted bread, then layer on the lettuce, sliced turkey, cheese, and potato chips. Top with another mayo-slathered slice of bread. Give the sandwich a little press to crunch the chips and hold everything together. Pickles of any kind make a great addition.

**Note:** This sandwich can be served hot with melty cheddar, but I prefer to smoke the turkey ahead of time, let it cool overnight in the fridge, and serve it cold. It's meant to be a refreshing sandwich, perfect for on-the-go.

# CRANBERRY BRIE TURKEY MELT

**MAKES 4 SANDWICHES**
**EQUIPMENT: SKILLET OR GRIDDLE**

**FOR CRANBERRY CHIMICHURRI:**

½ cup (30 g) finely chopped flat-leaf parsley

½ cup (8 g) finely chopped cilantro

4 cloves garlic, finely chopped or minced

½ cup (60 g) chopped dried cranberries

2 teaspoons dried oregano

2 teaspoons crushed red pepper flakes

¼ cup (59 ml) red wine vinegar, plus more as needed

1 cup (267 ml) extra virgin olive oil

1 teaspoon kosher salt, plus more as needed

Coarsely ground black pepper to taste

¼ cup (56 g) softened butter, for toasting

8 slices bread (see bread recommendations)

1½ pounds (680 g) Smoked Turkey Breast (p. 78), sliced thin

8-ounce (227 g) wedge Brie, sliced

½ red onion, thinly sliced

**BREAD RECOMMENDATIONS:**

Ciabatta

Sourdough

Focaccia

Baguette

French loaf

**This sandwich exists to showcase one of my favorite condiments: cranberry chimichurri. I first made it years ago as a remix to the classic, serving it with smoked turkey on sliders for Thanksgiving. This chimichurri has been my most requested recipe ever since, even at live events, because the herby, tangy sauce pairs perfectly with peppery smoked turkey. Combine that with the richness of melted Brie and the sharp bite of red onion, and you've got a sandwich that's so good, it might just get its own club. Sandwich joke, get it?**

**1.** Prepare the chimichurri first. Be sure to hand-chop the herbs and cranberries to retain their texture. Add the parsley, cilantro, garlic, cranberries, oregano, chili flakes, and red wine vinegar to a bowl. Using a fork, mix the ingredients while slowly drizzling in the olive oil. Add enough oil to fully coat and submerge the herbs, but not so much that they're drowning. Taste and adjust with salt, pepper, and more vinegar if needed. Store in the fridge, where it will stay fresh for about a week. It may lose its vibrant color over time, but the flavor will deepen.

**2.** Set out your other ingredients and preheat a large cast-iron skillet or griddle over medium-low heat. If using a skillet, you may need to cook the sandwiches two at a time given the amount of space.

**3.** Spread butter on the sliced bread and add to the hot pan, toasting for about 3 minutes or until golden brown. Repeat with the remaining bread and set aside.

**4.** Add the rest of the butter to the pan. Once it's melted, add a pile of the turkey slices. Warm the turkey for about 2 minutes on one side, then carefully flip the stack. Add slices of Brie and cover the pan with a lid to melt the cheese. Remove the turkey and transfer it to the toasted bread. Repeat for the remaining sandwiches.

**5.** Top the melted Brie with thin slices of red onion and a spoonful or two of chimichurri, then press the toasted top slice of bread into the sandwich. Serve immediately—because, let's be honest, you won't wait!

# SMOKIN' HOT RACHEL

**MAKES 4 SANDWICHES**
**EQUIPMENT: SKILLET OR GRIDDLE**

Hot Honey Mustard Sauce (p. 21)

8 slices bread (see bread recommendations)

8 slices Swiss cheese

1½ pounds (680 g) Smoked Turkey Breast (p. 78), sliced thin

1 cup (70 g) Crispy Sandwich Slaw (p. 167)

2 tablespoons (28 g) softened butter, for toasting

**BREAD RECOMMENDATIONS:**

Jewish rye bread

Caraway rye bread

Thin-sliced sourdough

French baguette

**The first time I had this was at a posh sandwich shop near my college campus, and I thought they were being cheeky with the name. Loosely based on the Reuben, this Rachel sandwich swaps out the sauerkraut and pastrami for crispy slaw and deli-sliced turkey. I've been making my own versions of it over the years—mainly because I can't get enough of home-made smoked turkey breast. And let's be real, it's so good that you might just forget about the original Reuben altogether. That might be extreme, but seriously, make this.**

**1.** Set out your ingredients and preheat a large cast-iron skillet or griddle over medium-low heat. If using a skillet, you may need to cook the sandwiches in batches depending on the amount of space in your skillet.

**2.** Spread the Hot Honey Mustard Sauce on each slice of bread.

**3.** On half of the slices, layer a slice of Swiss cheese, thin slices of smoked turkey, ¼ cup (18 g) of the slaw, and a second slice of Swiss cheese. Top with the remaining bread slices, sauce-side down. Use half of the butter to spread on the top of each sandwich.

**4.** Once the skillet or griddle is preheated, place the sandwiches butter-side down in the pan and toast the bread for about 3 minutes, until golden brown. While they toast, butter the top of each sandwich with the rest of softened butter. Flip the sandwiches and grill the other side until golden and crispy.

**5.** Remove the pan from the heat and cover with a lid to help melt the cheese. Once both sides are perfectly toasted and melty, remove the sandwiches. Serve them while warm and crispy—I told you the hype is real!

4

# PIT PERFECTION: FLAVORS THAT TAKE TIME

# ARGENTINE PULLED PORK WITH CHIMICHURRI SLAW

**SERVES ABOUT 12 TO 16**
**EQUIPMENT: SMOKER**

- 1 pork shoulder butt, about 7 to 10 pounds (3.2 to 4.5 kg)
- ½ cup (100 g) Prime Smoke Rub (p. 173), plus more as needed

**FOR CHIMICHURRI:**

- 1 cup (60 g) minced parsley
- ¼ cup (59 ml) red wine vinegar, plus more as needed
- 2 tablespoons (6 g) dried oregano
- 2 garlic cloves, finely chopped or minced
- 2 teaspoons crushed red pepper
- 1 teaspoon kosher salt, plus more as needed
- Coarsely ground black pepper to taste
- 1 cup (267 ml) olive oil

**FOR ARGENTINE SLAW:**

- 1 head green cabbage, finely shredded on a mandolin or by hand
- 1 sweet onion, finely sliced on a mandolin or by hand
- 1 large carrot, peeled and grated on the large holes of a box grater
- ½ cup (100 g) white sugar
- ½ cup (150 g) kosher salt

- Kosher salt, as needed
- 12 to 16 burger buns (see bread recommendations)
- Softened butter, for toasting
- Fresh Mayonnaise (p. 157)
- Tomatoes, sliced
- 12 to 16 slices provolone cheese

**When it comes to Argentine barbecue, it's all about letting the meat shine with minimal seasoning and maximum flavor. It's a lot like Texas BBQ: simple rubs, slow smoke, and a perfect bark that lets the meat shine with pure, smoky flavor. I've taken that no-nonsense approach and created a pulled pork sandwich that's anything but ordinary. The juicy, tender pork is the star, but that chimichurri slaw and fresh tomato? They bring out the best in every bite. This isn't just a sandwich; it's a moment to share with friends, good times, and great food.**

**1.** Remove the pork shoulder from the packaging and pat it dry with paper towels. Score shallow, diagonal cuts across the fat cap, then score at a 90-degree angle to create a crosshatch pattern. Season the pork evenly on all sides, and let it rest at room temperature while your smoker heats up. If possible, season the pork butt the night before and rest in the fridge uncovered which will promote a deeper flavor and crusty bark!

**2.** Prepare the chimichurri. Add all of the ingredients except for the oil to a bowl. Using a fork, mix the ingredients while slowly drizzling in the olive oil. Add enough oil to fully coat and submerge the herbs, but not so much that they're drowning. Taste and adjust with salt, pepper, and more vinegar if needed. Store in the fridge, where it will stay fresh for about a week. It may lose its vibrant color over time, but the flavor will deepen.

**CONTINUED** 

## ARGENTINE PULLED PORK WITH CHIMICHURRI SLAW, CONTINUED

**3.** Preheat the smoker to 265°F (129°C). Once your smoker has reached temperature, place the pork inside with the fat cap facing up. Allow it to smoke undisturbed for about 5 to 6 hours until the internal temperature reaches around 165°F to 170°F (74°C to 77°C). The time may vary depending on the size.

**4.** For the slaw, combine shredded cabbage, sliced onion, grated carrots, sugar, and salt in a large bowl, tossing to coat. Let it rest for 5 minutes, then transfer it to a colander or strainer and rinse thoroughly under cold running water. Dry the cabbage mix with a salad spinner, or layer it between paper towels on a baking sheet to blot dry.

**5.** Return the slaw mixture to the large bowl and add 1 cup (260 g) of the chimichurri, tossing with everything to coat. Add more as needed, tasting along the way. Store in the fridge until ready to use.

**6.** Check on the pork to see if it has reached the target temperature. Place heavy-duty foil on your workstation, overlapping two sheets. Remove the pork from the smoker and place it onto a sheet of foil. Tightly wrap it up in the foil, folding in the sides as you go to make sure it's sealed. Double-wrap it with the second sheet of foil, and throw it back in the smoker. Bump the heat up to 300°F (149°C).

**7.** Cook the pork for another 2 to 3 hours until it hits about 200°F (93°C). Start checking with a meat thermometer—it should feel like you're sticking the probe into a jar of peanut butter, with barely any resistance. Keep it going until it feels tender, then pull it from the smoker and let it rest wrapped for at least an hour before shredding.

**8.** When you're ready, pull out that bone and shred the meat. Season the pork with a little of the chimichurri and salt as needed. Toast the buns with butter. Assemble the buns with mayonnaise, slices of tomato, a warm pile of pork, provolone cheese, and the slaw. Dig in—this is a juicy one!

# BUFFALO PORK RIBWICH

**MAKES 6 TO 8 SANDWICHES**
**EQUIPMENT: SMOKER**

2 racks baby back pork ribs

¼ cup (56 g) Sweet Smolder Rub (p. 174)

**FOR BLUE CHEESE DRESSING:**

¼ cup (60 g) Fresh Mayonnaise (p. 157)

¼ cup (60 g) sour cream

3 tablespoons (45 ml) buttermilk

2 tablespoons (30 ml) white vinegar

2 cloves garlic, minced

¾ cup (90 g) crumbled blue cheese

Freshly ground black pepper

**FOR BLUE CHEESE SLAW:**

2 cups (140 g) thinly shaved cabbage

4 stalks pickled celery (make using the Master Brine for Quick Pickling on p. 181), cut on the bias

½ cup (120 g) Blue Cheese Dressing (above), plus more as needed

2 tablespoons (16 g) crushed pistachios

Coarsely ground pepper and salt to taste

Blue cheese crumbles, as needed

6 tablespoons (84 g) unsalted butter, cut into 6 pats, divided

2 cups (473 ml) Buffalo BBQ Sauce (p. 160)

6 to 8 buns or rolls (see bread recommendations)

Softened butter or Fresh Mayonnaise (p. 157), for toasting

**BREAD RECOMMENDATIONS:**

Sesame buns

Potato buns

Brioche buns

Buttermilk buns

Hoagie rolls

**If you've ever smoked ribs and twisted the bones out, you've probably wondered, *Should I make a sandwich with this?* Consider this your official green light. Rich, spicy, sweet, and smoky, this pork-packed sandwich has it all. It's surprisingly simple—easier than pulled pork—and delivers even more crispy bark textures. For the ultimate indulgence, pile it high with crispy blue cheese slaw and finish it off with a glaze of spicy Buffalo BBQ Sauce. You're welcome.**

**1.** Fire up the smoker to 250°F (121°C). Prep the ribs by removing the membrane—use a butter knife or a paper towel to make it easier. Using a small knife, remove any of the cartilage or small bones from the ends of the ribs. Dust the ribs with the rub on all sides. Once the smoker is ready, toss them in and let them smoke for about 3 hours, or until they reach around 165°F to 170°F (74°C to 77°C).

**2.** In a small bowl, mix up the Blue Cheese Dressing ingredients and season it to taste. For the slaw, toss the vegetable ingredients in a bowl with the pistachios, and add the Blue Cheese Dressing while tossing to evenly coat. Add more dressing or blue cheese crumbles if desired, then pop it in the fridge to chill while the ribs are smoking.

CONTINUED →

## BUFFALO PORK RIBWICH, CONTINUED

**3.** After about 3 hours in the smoker, once the ribs have developed a nice bark, pull them out. Lay out two large sheets of heavy-duty foil, place the ribs meat-side down, and add 3 pats of butter to the back. Wrap the ribs tightly, making sure the seam is on top and the bones aren't poking through the foil. Repeat with the second rack, then return the ribs to the smoker for another 90 minutes.

**4.** Check the ribs, pulling gently at the bones. They should be wiggly, which means they will slide out when finished. Open the foil into a boat and carefully flip the ribs so the meat is facing up. Smoke the ribs for another 30 minutes to crisp up the bark.

**5.** Once the ribs are around 200°F to 205°F (93°C to 96°C) and probe-tender, wrap the ribs back up in the foil and remove them from the smoker. Allow them to rest for about 30 minutes before tugging out the bones and slicing to the width of the bread.

**6.** You can glaze the ribs with the BBQ sauce and set them back on the smoker, or simply brush it on and serve. Lightly toast the buns with butter or mayonnaise before serving. Add a little dressing to the bottom slice, top it with the glazed ribs and slaw, and close it up. It's ready for you to crush!

# CAJUN BAYOU DIP

**MAKES 6 TO 8 SANDWICHES**
**EQUIPMENT: SMOKER AND SKILLET**

1 chuck roast, about 3 to 4 pounds (1.4 to 1.8 kg)
3 tablespoons (45 ml) Worcestershire sauce, divided
⅓ cup (67 g) Prime Smoke Rub (p. 173)
½ tablespoon (4 g) paprika
1 teaspoon dried oregano
1 teaspoon cayenne pepper

2 tablespoons (28 g) butter
2 ribs celery, diced
1 sweet onion, diced
1 green bell pepper, diced
2 garlic cloves, minced
2 cups (473 ml) beef broth
4 sprigs fresh thyme
12 to 14 ounces (340 to 397 g) smoked Andouille sausage

12 to 16 slices provolone cheese
6 to 8 rolls or hoagies (see recommendations)
Louisiana-style hot sauce

**BREAD RECOMMENDATIONS:**
French rolls
Italian rolls
Baguettes

**Smoking and braising meats opens up a whole world of flavor possibilities. I've made Mississippi pot roast plenty of times, but I was craving something with a little more punch. Adding spicy Andouille sausage and the Cajun trinity (peppers, onions, and celery) creates layers of savory and smoky goodness that seep into that rich beef. And let's be real, it also makes the best dipping sauce, so be sure to strain it and serve on the side. Each bite is packed with textures, heat, smoke, and deep flavor. Oh, and it's pretty messy—so unless you want to wear beef stains for the rest of the day, grab a bib.**

**1.** Preheat the smoker to 250°F (121°C). Rub the chuck roast with 1 tablespoon (15 ml) of the Worcestershire sauce as a binder. Combine the rub with paprika, oregano, and cayenne pepper, then season the chuck roast generously on all sides. Let the beef rest at room temperature while the smoker warms up. Place the beef in the smoker and cook for about 3 hours, or until it reaches an internal temperature of around 165°F (74°C).

**2.** While the beef is smoking, prepare the ingredients for the braise. Heat a skillet over medium heat and melt the butter. Add the diced celery, onion, and bell pepper, and cook for about 2 to 3 minutes. Add the garlic and cook for another 2 to 3 minutes until the vegetables are slightly softened and translucent. Remove from the heat and set aside.

**CONTINUED →**

## CAJUN BAYOU DIP, CONTINUED

**3.** Check the chuck roast. Once it reaches the target temperature, place it in a foil pan with the sauteed vegetable mix, beef broth, remaining 2 tablespoons (30 ml) of Worcestershire sauce, fresh thyme, and sausage. Wrap the top tightly with heavy-duty foil and add it back to the smoker and increase the heat to 275°F (135°C). Cook for an hour, then open the foil pan and flip the beef. Cover it again and continue to cook for another 1 to 2 hours, or until the meat reaches around 205°F (96°C) and is probe-tender. Timing may vary depending on the size of the chuck roast and its fat marbling. Once it's done, remove the pan and let the beef rest, covered, for 30 to 45 minutes, or until it's cool enough to handle.

**4.** Remove the chuck roast and sausages from the pan and discard the fresh thyme. Strain the cooked vegetables and peppers, keeping the juices in a separate bowl. Return the veggies and peppers to the foil pan. Place the chuck roast back in the pan and shred the meat, discarding any unwanted fat. Add a little of the reserved juices to moisten the meat. Slice the sausages into small coins and add them to the beef and veggies. Stir everything together—it's time to build the sandwiches.

**5.** Tear pieces of sliced provolone and place them on the bread, followed by a generous pile of the smoked meats. Add more cheese on top if desired, and drizzle with hot sauce. Serve these warm sandwiches with a bowl of the spicy broth on the side for dunking.

# PULLED HAM PARTY SANDWICH

**SERVES ABOUT 8 TO 10**
**EQUIPMENT: SMOKER**

**FOR SMOKED HAM RUB:**

½ cup (115 g) brown sugar
3 tablespoons (21 g) paprika
2 tablespoons (12 g) coarsely ground black pepper
1 tablespoon (9 g) granulated garlic
1 tablespoon (8 g) chili powder
1 teaspoon ground ginger
1 teaspoon ground cinnamon

1 bone-in, whole ham shank (not spiral), about 7 to 10 pounds (3.2 to 4.5 kg)
¼ cup (44 g) yellow mustard
Smoked Ham Rub (recipe at right)
½ cup (118 ml) beer, pineapple juice, or apple juice

**FOR BROWN SUGAR DIJON SAUCE:**

½ cup or 1 stick (112 g) butter, melted
2 tablespoons (30 g) brown sugar
2 tablespoons (22 g) Dijon mustard
2 tablespoons (30 ml) Worcestershire sauce

8 to 10 rolls (see bread recommendations)
Fresh Mayonnaise (p. 157)
Candied Jalapeños (p. 177)
8 to 10 slices Gruyère or Swiss cheese
Poppy seeds, optional

**BREAD RECOMMENDATIONS:**

Poppy seed buns
Kaiser rolls
Onion buns
Brioche buns
Portuguese rolls

Smoked pulled ham is seriously underrated, so I set out to fix that by transforming one of my favorite ham sandwiches, even if it comes with a pretty depressing name: funeral sandwiches. We're talking smoky, tender ham piled with candied jalapeños and rich cheese, glazed and baked in the oven to create a crispy, sweet top. Taking a bite feels almost like dessert, but then those spicy jalapeños and smoky bark bite back. Before you know it, you're realizing you're eating the best ham sandwich of your life. Trust me, no tears over this one.

**1.** Start by mixing all of the ham rub ingredients in a small bowl. Remove the ham from its packaging and pat it dry with paper towels. Rub a thin layer of yellow mustard over the entire surface of the ham, excluding the flat cut side (the bottom). Generously sprinkle the seasoning over the mustard-covered surface.

**2.** Preheat the smoker to 250°F (121°C). Place the ham in the smoker, cut side down, and let it cook for about 2 to 4 hours, or until it reaches an internal temperature of 165°F to 170°F (74°C to 77°C).

**CONTINUED** →

## PULLED HAM PARTY SANDWICH, CONTINUED

**3.** Once the ham is done, remove it from the smoker and transfer it to a foil pan. Add the beer, pineapple juice, or apple juice to the bottom of the pan, then double-wrap the ham with heavy-duty aluminum foil.

**4.** Increase the smoker temperature to 300°F (149°C), then return the wrapped foil pan to the smoker. Continue cooking for another 2 to 4 hours, or until the ham reaches probe tenderness, around 200°F to 208°F (93°C to 98°C).

**5.** Once the ham is ready, remove it from the smoker and let it rest on the counter, still wrapped. Allow it to rest for at least 30 to 40 minutes. Shred the meat.

**6.** Mix up the ingredients for the Brown Sugar Dijon Sauce in a small bowl. Preheat the oven to 350°F (177°C). Start assembling the sandwiches by spreading a little mayo on each bun, then layering with jalapeños, ham, and cheese. Top with the other bun and brush on the buttery glaze, then sprinkle with poppy seeds (if using). Repeat for the remaining sandwiches and place them on a baking sheet.

**7.** Bake for 12 to 15 minutes, or until the buns are toasted and slightly crisp on top.

**8.** Remove from the oven and serve warm. The top will slightly shatter as you take a bite, revealing the melty cheese and juicy ham inside.

# SPICY PORK DIPS

**SERVES ABOUT 12 TO 16**
**EQUIPMENT: SMOKER**

1 pork shoulder butt, about 7 to 10 pounds (3.2 to 4.5 kg)

½ cup (111 g) Sweet Smolder Rub (p. 174), plus more as needed

1 tablespoon (5 g) ground cayenne pepper

**FOR SPICY MOP SAUCE:**

½ cup or 1 stick (112 g) unsalted butter

2 cups (473 ml) chicken broth

½ cup (188 ml) apple cider vinegar

½ cup (188 ml) white vinegar

2 tablespoons (40 g) honey

¼ cup (59 ml) Louisiana-style hot sauce, plus more as needed

2 tablespoons (30 ml) Worcestershire sauce

2 tablespoons (10 g) finely ground black pepper

2 tablespoons (10 g) ground cayenne pepper

Salt to taste

12 to 16 slider rolls (see bread recommendations)

Pickles for serving

**BREAD RECOMMENDATIONS:**

Brioche slider rolls

Potato slider rolls

White slider rolls

Hawaiian slider rolls

**Grilled pork from Monroe County, Kentucky, might be the best regional barbecue you've never heard of. Pork steaks and chops are cooked over charcoal and dunked in a spicy vinegar dip that really slaps. I knew I had to bring that magic to the table in a way that everyone could get in on. These handheld spicy pork dips are irresistible and easy to share. Smoked pork shoulder is shredded and stacked on slider buns, then dunked into that spicy, tangy mop sauce that's got just the right kick without stealing the natural flavors from the pork. This dish is all about that slow-cooked pork, bold heat, and the joy of sharing a killer meal with the crew.**

**1.** Remove the pork shoulder from the packaging and pat it dry with paper towels. Score shallow, diagonal cuts across the fat cap, then score at a 90-degree angle to create a crosshatch pattern. Mix the Sweet Smolder Rub with the cayenne, and season the pork evenly on all sides. Let the pork sit at room temperature while your smoker warms up. If possible, season the pork butt the night before and rest in the fridge uncovered—this promotes a deeper flavor and better bark!

**2.** Preheat the smoker to 265°F (129°C). Once your smoker has reached temperature, place the pork inside with the fat cap facing up.

CONTINUED 

## SPICY PORK DIPS, CONTINUED

**3.** Next, prepare the mop sauce. Warm up all the ingredients in a saucepan over medium heat on the stove, letting it simmer for about 10 minutes. Taste it, and adjust with a bit of salt or extra heat if needed. You want this sauce to be tangy and spicy, with a touch of sweetness to balance it out. Keep over very low heat; it'll be used for mopping the warm pork.

**4.** After 2 hours of smoking the pork, gently mop some of that sauce over the pork's fat cap. Keep mopping once an hour until the pork reaches around 165°F to 170°F (74°C to 77°C), which should take about 5 to 6 hours, depending on the size of your shoulder. Set aside the rest of that mop sauce—you'll need it for dipping later.

**5.** Place the foil on your workstation, overlapping the two sheets. Once the pork reaches the target temperature, remove it from the smoker and place it onto a sheet of foil. Mop the pork one last time, then tightly wrap it up in the foil, folding in the sides as you go to make sure it's sealed. Double-wrap it with the second sheet of foil, and throw it back in the smoker. Bump the heat up to 300°F (149°C).

**6.** Cook the pork for another 2 to 3 hours until it hits about 200°F (93°C). Start checking with a meat thermometer—it should feel like you're sticking the probe into a jar of peanut butter, with barely any resistance. Keep it going until it feels tender, then pull it from the smoker and let it rest wrapped for at least an hour before shredding.

**7.** When you're ready, pull out that bone and shred the meat. Stir in about ⅓ cup (79 ml) of the mop sauce, taste it, and add more if you need. Serve the pulled pork on toasted slider buns with pickles and a bowl of the warm mop sauce. Make sure you have plenty of napkins and cold beverages on hand.

# CHOPPED PORK AND PUB CHEESE

**SERVES ABOUT 8 TO 10**
**EQUIPMENT: SMOKER AND BLENDER**

- 4 pounds (1.8 kg) country-style pork ribs
- ½ cup (111 g) Sweet Smolder Rub (p. 174), plus more as needed

**FOR PUB CHEESE:**

- 3 cups (338 g) shredded cheddar cheese
- 4 ounces (113 g) cream cheese, softened
- 1 clove garlic
- 1 tablespoon (15 ml) Worcestershire sauce
- 1 tablespoon (11 g) Dijon mustard
- 1 tablespoon (9 g) chipotles in adobo sauce
- ⅔ cups (158 ml) flat beer, room temperature
- Freshly ground black pepper
- Kosher salt
- 2 tablespoons (6 g) diced chives

- Apple cider vinegar, for spritzing
- 8 to 10 burger buns or rolls (see bread recommendations)
- Softened butter, for toasting
- Hot Honey Mustard Sauce (p. 21)

**BREAD RECOMMENDATIONS:**

- Pretzel buns
- Onion buns
- Portuguese rolls
- Seeded buns

**Looking for a solid excuse to eat creamy pub cheese? Well, here it is. Crispy, slow-smoked pork gets piled high on top of tangy, spicy hot honey mustard, then smothered in velvety beer cheese. That'll have your taste buds doing a happy dance! This award-winning sauce helped me snag a local BBQ competition win, and now I'm sharing it with you (you're welcome). Pair it with some Fresh Pickles (p. 178) or Crispy Sandwich Slaw (p. 167) to cut through the richness and balance out the flavors. This sandwich is a game-changer.**

**1.** Preheat the smoker to 265°F (129°C). Prepare the ribs by removing any excess fat or loose bones (we'll be chopping up the meat to serve later). Season the meat generously with the rub on all sides and place it in the smoker once it reaches the target temperature. Allow the pork to smoke for about 3 hours undisturbed.

**2.** While the pork is cooking, prepare the Pub Cheese sauce. Using a high-speed blender, add the cheddar, cream cheese, garlic, Worcestershire sauce, Dijon, and chipotles. Press everything down slightly and turn the blender on medium-low. Slowly pour in the beer, adding most of it before turning the speed of the blender up higher.

**3.** Blend until the cheese sauce is smooth, using more beer if necessary. The cheese sauce should be fully blended, light, and airy. Taste and adjust with salt and pepper as needed. Pour the sauce into a container and stir in the diced chives. Store in the fridge until use.

**CONTINUED** 

## CHOPPED PORK AND PUB CHEESE, CONTINUED

**4.** Check the pork ribs—they should be around 165°F to 175°F (74°C to 79°C) with a nice, developed bark. Lightly spritz the edges with some apple cider vinegar, flipping the pork pieces as you go. Keep cooking for another 45 to 60 minutes, or until the meat is probe-tender. Typically, that'll be around the 190°F to 200°F (88°C to 93°C) mark, but use your meat thermometer and your gut here—pork varies based on size and fat content.

**5.** Once the ribs are tender, pull them off the smoker and place them in a foil pan. Cover with plastic wrap to allow the ribs to rest and steam. This step helps lock in the flavor and keeps things juicy.

**6.** Lightly toast the buns to golden brown with some softened butter in a warm pan for a few minutes.

**7.** Chop up the pork, removing any small bones, and get ready to build the sandwich. Spread some honey mustard on the bottom bun, pile on the chopped pork, and top with a generous dollop of beer cheese sauce. Smash down the top bun and dig in.

**8.** Hopefully you picked up some extra beer—you're definitely going to want a cold one to go with this.

**Note:** Prep the meat the night before to allow it to absorb the seasoning more deeply. This also helps the pork develop a crispier crust, similar to carnitas, as the air in the fridge dries out the surface. For the best results, dry-brine the meat on a baking sheet with a wire rack.

# CARNITAS TORTA

**SERVES ABOUT 8 TO 10**
**EQUIPMENT: SMOKER**

- 4 pounds (1.8 kg) country-style pork ribs
- 3 tablespoons (45 g) brown sugar
- 1 tablespoon (6 g) coarsely ground black pepper
- 2 tablespoons (36 g) kosher salt
- 1½ teaspoons granulated garlic
- 1 teaspoon onion powder
- 1 teaspoon ground Mexican oregano
- ½ teaspoon ground cumin
- ½ teaspoon ground coriander
- ¼ teaspoon ground cinnamon
- Apple cider vinegar, for spritzing

- 8 to 10 rolls (see bread recommendations)
- Sour Cream Sandwich Sauce (p. 159)
- Tomatoes, sliced
- Pickled Jalapeños (p. 182)
- ½ head green cabbage, finely shredded on a mandolin or by hand
- Guacamole Spread (p. 159)

**BREAD RECOMMENDATIONS:**

- Torta bread
- Telera rolls
- Kaiser rolls
- Potato buns

**If you've never had carnitas, imagine pieces of pork slowly cooked in their own fat with citrus, spices, and sometimes a splash of cola. After hours of cooking, the meat turns golden and crispy on the outside, with an impossibly juicy center. It's one of my all-time favorite meats, so I had to find a way to bring that magic to the smoker while staying true to the essence of carnitas. This rub nails it, blending sweet and warming flavors with savory spices that bring out the best of the pork. Pile up that crispy, juicy meat on your favorite roll, add a few fresh toppings, and you'll see why this is worth whipping up.**

**1.** Prepare the ribs by removing any excess fat or loose bones (we'll be chopping up the meat to serve later). Mix the herbs and spices together to make the rub and generously season the meat on all sides.

**2.** Preheat the smoker to 265°F (129°C). Once it reaches the target temperature, place the meat in the smoker. Allow the pork to smoke for about 3 hours, undisturbed.

**3.** Check the pork ribs—they should be around 165°F to 175°F (74°C to 79°C), with a nicely developed bark. Lightly spritz the edges with apple cider vinegar, flipping the pork pieces as you go. Continue cooking for another 45 to 60 minutes, or until the meat is probe-tender. Typically, this will be around 190°F to 200°F (88°C to 93°C), but trust your meat thermometer and your gut here—pork varies based on size and fat content.

**4.** Once the ribs are tender, pull them off the smoker and place them in a foil pan. Cover with plastic wrap to allow the ribs to rest and steam for about 30 minutes. This step helps lock in the flavor and keeps things juicy.

**5.** Remove any bones and shred or chop up the meat when ready to serve. Slice the torta bread and add the sour cream sauce, tomatoes, jalapeños, meat, cabbage, and guac spread. Press down that bun and dig into a crispy, juicy sandwich.

# SWEET AND SOUR PULLED PORK

**MAKES 12 TO 14 SANDWICHES**
**EQUIPMENT: SMOKER**

1 pork shoulder butt, about 7 to 10 pounds (3.2 to 4.5 kg)
⅓ cup (100 g) kosher salt
¼ cup (28 g) paprika
¼ cup (60 g) brown sugar
1 tablespoon (6 g) coarsely ground black pepper
1 tablespoon (7 g) Chinese five-spice
½ tablespoon (1 g) ground coriander
2 teaspoons mustard powder
2 teaspoons granulated garlic
1 teaspoon cayenne powder

2 red bell peppers
2 green bell peppers
1 red onion
1 can (20 ounces [567 g]) pineapple slices, drained

**FOR SWEET AND SOUR SAUCE:**
¼ cup (60 g) ketchup
½ cup (118 ml) apple cider vinegar
¼ cup (118 ml) Shaoxing wine or dry sherry
½ cup (115 g) brown sugar
1 tablespoon (15 ml) Worcestershire sauce
4 teaspoons (11 g) cornstarch
1 teaspoon salt, plus more as needed

1 tablespoon (15 ml) neutral oil
12 to 14 buns or rolls (see bread recommendations)
Fresh Mayonnaise (p. 157)
½ cup (50 g) scallions, thinly sliced

**BREAD RECOMMENDATIONS:**
Potato buns
Brioche buns
Kaiser rolls
Sesame buns

Growing up, sweet and sour chicken or pork was one of my favorite American-Chinese dishes. I couldn't handle the spicy chiles back then, so this was my go-to. Bringing those flavors into the world of barbecue works so well, especially because smoked pork pairs perfectly with a tangy, sweet sauce. The unique spice blend uses warming spices and sugar to create a crusty, savory bark on the outside of the pork. Pile the shredded meat on a soft bun and then load it up with peppers, onions, pineapple, and more sauce for a flavor explosion that any backyard pitmaster can get behind. This recipe also tastes great with smoked pulled chicken. If that's your thing, be sure to refer to the earlier recipe (p. 41).

**1.** Pat dry the pork shoulder with paper towels. Score shallow, diagonal cuts across the fat cap, then score at a 90-degree angle to create a crosshatch pattern. Combine the salt, paprika, brown sugar, black pepper, Chinese five-spice, coriander, mustard powder, granulated garlic, and cayenne to make the seasoning and generously apply it to all sides of the pork (you may have some left over).

**2.** Preheat the smoker to 265°F (129°C). Once your smoker has reached temperature, place the pork inside with the fat cap facing up. Allow it to smoke undisturbed for about 5 to 6 hours until the internal temperature reaches around 165°F to 170°F (74°C to 77°C). The time may vary depending on the size.

**CONTINUED** →

# SWEET AND SOUR PULLED PORK, CONTINUED

**3.** Slice the bell peppers and onions into strips and set them aside. Cut the pineapple rings in thirds. Set aside.

**4.** Combine all the sauce ingredients in a medium saucepan and bring to a simmer. Whisk the sauce until it thickens, which should take about 5 minutes. Remove from heat and set aside.

**5.** Place the foil on your workstation, overlapping two sheets. Once the pork reaches the target temperature, remove it from the smoker and place it onto a sheet of foil. Tightly wrap it up in the foil, folding in the sides as you go to make sure it's sealed. Double-wrap it with the second sheet of foil, and throw it back in the smoker. Bump the heat up to 300°F (149°C).

**6.** Cook the pork for another 2 to 3 hours until it hits about 200°F (93°C). Start checking with a meat thermometer—it should feel like you're sticking the probe into a jar of peanut butter, with barely any resistance. Keep it going until it feels tender, then pull it from the smoker and let it rest wrapped for at least an hour before shredding.

**7.** Heat the oil in a skillet over medium-high heat. Toss in the peppers and onions, giving them a good stir with tongs to coat them in the oil. Let them cook for a few minutes until they start to soften and get a nice char. Stir them around, then throw in the pineapple slices. Keep cooking and stirring for about 3 to 4 minutes, then turn off the heat. Pour in some of that Sweet and Sour Sauce, and toss everything together to get a good coating.

**8.** Remove the bone from the pork butt and shred the meat. Season with a little more of the rub and a few tablespoons of the sauce. If you're using soft buns, you can hit them with a little fresh mayo and toast them in a pan before serving.

**9.** Serve up the sandwiches with the toasted buns, mayo, pulled pork, peppers and onion mix, a little extra sauce, then finish it off with the scallions.

# PHILLY-STYLE SMOKED RIBWICH

**SERVES ABOUT 6 TO 8**
**EQUIPMENT: SMOKER**

2 racks baby back pork ribs

¼ cup (50 g) Prime Smoke Rub (p. 173)

1 tablespoon (4 g) fresh thyme, minced

1 tablespoon (2 g) fresh rosemary, minced

Kosher salt as needed

2 pounds (907 g) broccoli rabe, trimmed and cut into 1-inch (2.5-cm) pieces

¼ cup (45 g) chopped jarred Italian long hot peppers or other spicy pickled peppers

2 garlic cloves, minced

Pinch chili flakes

6 tablespoons (84 g) unsalted butter, cut into 6 pats

6 to 8 large rolls (see bread recommendations)

12 to 16 slices provolone cheese

**BREAD RECOMMENDATIONS:**

Italian rolls

Seeded long roll

French bread

**This sandwich is a spin on the classic roast pork from Philly, keeping the core flavors and traditions while introducing the meaty, crusty goodness of a smoked rack of ribs. Sure, you could use a larger cut of pork and thinly slice it, but you'd be missing out on the crispy bark and those slow-smoked fatty bits that bring an explosion of flavors and textures. The slowly braised broccoli rabe soaks up the porky flavors, creating an earthy, spicy contrast to the rich pork and creamy provolone. Philly knows what's up, and this impossibly juicy combination is here to stay.**

**1.** Fire up the smoker to 250°F (121°C). Prep the ribs by removing the membrane—use a butter knife or a paper towel to make it easier. Using a small knife, remove any of the cartilage or small bones from the ends of the ribs. Combine the smoke rub with the minced thyme and rosemary. Season the ribs with the mixture on all sides. Once the smoker is ready, toss them in and let them smoke for about 3 hours, or until they reach around 165°F to 170°F (74°C to 77°C).

**2.** Add enough salt to a large pot of water so it is noticeably salty, similar to seawater; this helps to season the food during blanching. Bring the pot to a boil. Add the trimmed broccoli rabe in batches, blanching for about 2 minutes. Transfer to an ice bath to stop the cooking process. Once cooled, drain the broccoli and transfer it to a bowl with the chopped peppers, minced garlic, and chili flakes. Mix everything up and set aside—this will be added to the ribs later.

**3.** After about 3 hours in the smoker, once the ribs have developed a nice bark, pull them out. Lay out two large sheets of heavy-duty foil. Place the ribs on the foil meat-side down, and top with half of the broccoli rabe mixture and 3 pats of butter, cradled in the curve of the ribs. Wrap the rack tightly with both sheets of foil, making sure the seam is on top and the bones aren't poking through. Repeat with the second rack, then return the ribs to the smoker for another 90 minutes.

**CONTINUED** 

## PHILLY-STYLE SMOKED RIBWICH, CONTINUED

**4.** Carefully open the foil and check the ribs. They should be around 200°F to 205°F (93°C to 96°C) and probe-tender between the bones. If so, wrap the ribs back up and remove them from the smoker, allowing them to rest for about 30 to 45 minutes.

**5.** Unwrap the ribs and transfer the cooked broccoli rabe mixture to a bowl. Wiggle out the bones; they should pop out easily. Move the ribs to a cutting board and pour the remaining juices from the foil into a bowl. This is the good stuff. Slice the ribs to match the length of your bread.

**6.** Slice the bread open along the length, leaving a seam for folding. Hollow out a little of the bread from the center so the ribs fit comfortably inside. Tear pieces of sliced provolone and place them on the bread, followed by the tender ribs. Top with a healthy portion of the cooked broccoli rabe and a few spoonfuls of the juices. Press down gently to let the bread soak up some of the juices, then slice and serve.

**Note:** Do not stick the meat thermometer through the foil to check for tenderness, as you might accidentally pierce the bottom of the foil and drain all the buttery juices. Plus, you can't tell if you're poking meat or bone, so take your time and carefully open the foil to check.

# BIRRIA FIRE DIP

**MAKES 6 TO 8 SANDWICHES**
**EQUIPMENT: SMOKER AND DUTCH OVEN**

1 chuck roast, about 3 to 4 pounds (1.4 to 1.8 kg)

⅓ cup (67 g) Prime Smoke Rub (p. 173)

**FOR BIRRIA BROTH:**

6 dehydrated shiitake mushrooms

2½ cups (591 ml) warm water

6 dried guajillo chiles, stems and seeds removed

2 dried ancho chiles, stems and seeds removed

8 garlic cloves, diced

1 teaspoon dried thyme

1 teaspoon minced peeled ginger

2 tablespoons (30 ml) soy sauce

2 tablespoons (30 g) gochujang

2 cups (473 ml) beef broth

1 cup (235 ml) water, if needed

6 to 8 rolls

Softened butter, for toasting

Diced green onions

**BREAD RECOMMENDATIONS:**

Italian rolls

Sesame hoagie rolls

French bread

Torta bread

**Birria isn't a quickie meal—it's a flavor marathon. That's why I go big and make enough to feed a small army (or just me for the week). Sure, tacos are the authentic way to serve up this braised beef, but I've got a serious thing for that consommé. Spoiler alert: It makes the ultimate red-stained, drippy, mind-blowing sandwich. This version layers in flavors inspired by Japanese and Korean cuisine. It's savory, spicy, and guaranteed to get a little messy. Stock up on napkins!**

**1.** Preheat the smoker to 250°F (121°C). Trim any silverskin or hard pieces of fat from the outside of the chuck roast. Slice the roast into smaller portions, about 8 to 10 pieces, and season generously on all sides with the Prime Smoke Rub. Place them on the smoker and allow them to cook undisturbed for an hour.

**2.** Soak the mushrooms in the warm, not boiling, water for about 30 minutes until they are hydrated. Drain the liquid with a coffee filter or cheesecloth in a strainer over a bowl. Reserve this mushroom broth and set the shiitakes aside.

**3.** Wash the dried chile peppers in a bowl and cover with warm water (not the mushroom broth), covering the bowl with a towel to keep the steam in. Hydrate the chiles for about 10 to 15 minutes. Discard the water, and transfer the hydrated chiles to a blender with the mushroom broth, garlic, thyme, ginger, soy sauce, and gochujang. Blend until smooth, and add to a large Dutch oven along with beef broth.

**4.** Place the pot in the smoker, adding the smoked beef to the liquid. If needed, add water to ensure the beef is completely covered. Cover the Dutch oven and allow it to cook for about 3 to 3½ hours until the meat is fall-apart tender. Check on it periodically to adjust the beef and ensure it's not boiling too rapidly.

**5.** Once the beef is tender and shredded, strain out about 2 cups (473 ml) of broth and set aside in bowls. Slice the bread and lightly toast the buns to golden brown with some softened butter in a warm pan for a few minutes. Pile on the juicy shredded beef and serve with the reserved broth and green onions for garnish.

# OVERNIGHT BRISKET

**SERVES ABOUT 8 TO 10**
**EQUIPMENT: SMOKER**

- 1 whole packer brisket (about 12 to 14 pounds [5.4 to 6.4 kg])
- ½ cup (100 g) Prime Smoke Rub (p. 173), plus more as needed
- ¼ cup (50 g) beef tallow, melted, optional

**Note:** Every whole packer brisket will have slightly different-sized muscles and layers of fat. Knowing what to trim and where takes practice—that means you need to smoke more briskets!

**Smoking a brisket, especially if you're new to the world of barbecue, can feel like a big task. But over the years, I've come to realize that the Internet and cookbooks have overcomplicated the process. Brisket is actually pretty simple when you break it down into three main phases: smoking, wrapping, and resting. This overnight brisket guide is designed for the average person who doesn't want to spend their entire weekend stressing about the cook. It's flexible, straightforward, and will give you juicy, flavorful backyard brisket—perfect for sandwiches, tacos, wraps, and much more!**

**1.** Prepare the brisket in the afternoon, with the goal of smoking it overnight. This allows enough time to trim and season the brisket before placing it in the smoker as you head to bed—don't worry, you got this!

**2.** Start by trimming the brisket to remove excess fat. The goal is to create a clean, even surface for better cooking and bark formation without overtrimming the meat. It's easiest to do this step while the brisket is cold, right out of the fridge. Begin by trimming the sides, removing a thin strip of meat and fat to streamline the shape and expose the muscle structure. Once you can see the fat cap on top, focus on trimming it down to about ¼-inch (6-mm) thick. Remove the hard chunk of fat from the bottom, where the point and flat muscles meet.

**3.** Generously coat the brisket in Prime Smoke Rub, ensuring all surfaces are covered. Pat it into the meat to create a nice layer. For best results, let the brisket rest uncovered on a baking sheet in the fridge for at least an hour before placing it in the smoker. The cold temperature of the brisket will help the smoke adhere better and slow down the cooking process, ensuring you don't wake up to a fully cooked, dry brisket.

**4.** Preheat your smoker to 225°F (107°C). While you can use any type of smoker for this recipe, a pellet smoker makes it easy and hands-off, letting you smoke the brisket overnight with minimal monitoring.

**CONTINUED** →

## OVERNIGHT BRISKET, CONTINUED

**5.** Remove the brisket from the fridge and place it in the smoker, fat-side up. The goal is to let it smoke overnight for about 7 to 8 hours while you (hopefully) sleep. Smoke the brisket until it reaches an internal temperature of 165°F to 175°F (74°C to 79°C), depending on when the bark has developed to your liking. Ideally, it should be close to this temperature when you wake up.

**6.** Once the brisket hits the target temperature range, it's time to wrap it in pink butcher paper. Wrapping it will help retain moisture and speed up the cooking process, especially when smoking overnight. If you have beef tallow, you can warm it up and pour it over the brisket before wrapping. Roll out 2 large sheets of the butcher paper and overlap them. Place the brisket down and roll it tight, folding in the sides—make sure there's enough length to roll each side of the brisket twice.

**7.** Raise the smoker temperature to 275°F (135°C) and return the wrapped brisket to the smoker, fat-side up. Continue cooking until it's probe-tender, which should take 3 to 5 hours, depending on the size of the brisket and how well it's wrapped. Keep an eye on the internal temperature—when it reaches 200°F to 205°F (93°C to 96°C), the probe should slide in and out of the meat with little resistance, signaling it's time to rest.

**8.** Remove the wrapped brisket from the smoker and let it rest at room temperature, still wrapped, for at least 20 minutes. If you prefer, you can place it in an insulated cooler with towels or an oven set to a low temperature (140°F to 170°F [60°C to 77°C]). Resting allows the juices to redistribute throughout the meat. For best results, let it rest for at least 2 hours, though it can rest even longer if needed.

**9.** Slice the flat against the grain for thin slices that are perfect for sandwiches. The larger point muscle should be sliced in half lengthwise before slicing to serve. Be sure to trim off the ends of the point that are darker and tougher—these are perfect for making burnt ends (p. 126).

**Note:** Only slice what you plan to serve! Like any meat, brisket can dry out if presliced and stored as leftovers. Vacuum-sealing can help preserve the juiciness.

# KOREAN BRISKET MELT

**MAKES 2 SANDWICHES**
**EQUIPMENT: SKILLET OR GRIDDLE**

Korean Mayonnaise (p. 158)

1 pound (454 g) Overnight Brisket flat (p. 119), sliced thin

1 cup (142 g) drained chopped kimchi

2 tablespoons (28 g) butter

4 slices bread (see bread recommendations)

4 slices sharp cheddar cheese

**BREAD RECOMMENDATIONS:**

Jewish rye

Caraway seeded rye bread

Texas toast

Pullman loaf

Thin-sliced sourdough

**This is the sandwich that converted my wife from being a vegetarian (yep, it's possible). Kimchi was the gateway that bridged the gap, with its tangy, umami-packed flavors soaking into the tender slices of brisket. The sharp cheddar cuts through the richness of the smoky meat, creating a perfect balance. Together, this unexpected combo brings a wild mix of tangy, spicy, and smoky indulgence that demands to be devoured—immediately. This, my friends, is my wife's sandwich.**

**1.** Preheat the oven to 200°F (93°C) and set up a baking sheet with a wire rack.

**2.** Start by mixing up the Korean Mayonnaise ingredients. Adjust the mixture with more chili paste for extra heat or more brine if it's too thick. The goal is for it to be spreadable. Slather it on one side of each slice of bread.

**3.** Heat a skillet or griddle over medium-low heat. Add the slices of brisket and warm them through for 1 to 2 minutes, flipping as needed. Once warmed, remove the brisket and add the chopped kimchi, cooking it just enough to heat it through and reduce some of the liquid.

**4.** Remove the kimchi and add half of the butter to the skillet. When it melts, place one slice of bread, mayo side down, in the skillet. Top with a slice of cheddar, warm kimchi, sliced brisket, another slice of cheese, and the second slice of bread, mayo side up. Once the underside is golden brown, after about 3 minutes, flip the sandwich and add the remaining butter. Press down gently to ensure even toasting and help the cheese melt.

**5.** Once the bottom is perfectly browned, remove the sandwich and place it on the wire rack in the oven. Make the remaining sandwich and let them rest in the oven for 3 to 5 minutes before serving. This step helps prevent soggy bread and ensures extra melty cheddar goodness.

# BACKYARD BRISKET STACK

**MAKES 4 LARGE BURGERS**
**EQUIPMENT: SMOKER**

- 6 strips thick-cut bacon
- 1 white onion, sliced thin
- Kosher salt, to taste
- ½ pound (227 g) Overnight Brisket flat (p. 119), sliced thin
- 4 burger buns (see bread recommendations)
- 1 pound (454 g) ground beef, 80/20
- Freshly ground black pepper
- 4 slices cheddar cheese
- Fresh Mayonnaise (p. 157)
- House BBQ Sauce (p. 163)
- Fresh Pickles (p. 178) or Quick Pickles (p. 181)

**BREAD RECOMMENDATIONS:**

- Potato buns
- Brioche buns
- Kaiser rolls
- Sesame buns

**Everyone looks for a stack like this in a barbecue cookbook because we all want that visual confirmation that we're not alone in our desire to get messy and indulge. I'm here to show you how to get the most out of this combo of salty brisket, crispy bacon, tangy pickles, and spicy sauce, piled on top of tender beef, all wrapped in pillowy bread soaking up every last drip. If you love big, bold barbecue flavors, this burger is your new best friend.**

**1.** Heat a skillet or griddle over medium-low heat. Add the bacon and cook it slowly, flipping as needed to crisp up. Once crispy, remove the bacon and set it aside to drain on a paper towel.

**2.** Turn the heat up to medium and add the sliced onions. Lightly salt them to taste, and cook for about 4 to 5 minutes until they begin to brown and soften. Remove the onions from the pan and set them with the bacon to drain. Next, add the sliced brisket and cook for about 1 to 2 minutes; just enough to warm it through. Remove and set aside when ready.

**3.** Toast the buns in the remaining bacon and brisket juices—that's the good stuff!

**4.** Loosely form 4 equal patties from the ground beef, pressing gently in the center to prevent them from puffing up. Season both sides with salt and pepper, then add the patties to the hot skillet, leaving space between each one.

**5.** Cook the burgers until they're nicely seared and browned halfway up the sides. Flip the burgers and sear the other side, cooking to your preferred doneness. Once done, remove the pan from the heat, add a slice of cheese, and cover with a lid to help it melt.

**6.** Assemble the burger with a little mayo on the bottom bun, followed by onions, the cheeseburger patty, brisket, bacon, BBQ sauce, pickles, and the top bun. Have some paper towels handy—you know what to do.

# CHIPOTLE BURNT ENDS

**SERVES ABOUT 4 TO 6**
**EQUIPMENT: SMOKER**

- Burnt edges from 1 freshly smoked Overnight Brisket point (p. 119), sliced and cubed
- Prime Smoke Rub, as needed
- 1 cup (235 ml) Chipotle BBQ Sauce (p. 165), plus more for serving
- Brisket drippings, if reserved
- 4 to 6 buns (see bread recommendations)
- Fresh Pickles (p. 178) or Quick Pickles (p. 181)
- White onion, thinly sliced

**BREAD RECOMMENDATIONS:**

- Potato buns
- Brioche buns
- White bread
- Texas toast

**Burnt ends are the true "meat candy," little ruby-red gems that look almost too good to eat. Today, we'll slap them on a bun for the ultimate indulgence. The homemade spicy Chipotle BBQ Sauce adds a smoky, slightly sweet kick, with a deep, rich heat that lingers just enough to make you go back for more. With a crispy crunch on the outside and melt-in-your-mouth tenderness on the inside—this is the kind of treat that makes me forget my diet every time.**

**1.** Slice off the dark, crispy edges from the point of the brisket. If you don't have much, it's fine to add some extra thick slices of the point. Cut the meat into ½-inch (1-cm) cubes and place them in a foil pan.

**2.** Heat the smoker to 225°F (107°C). Dust some additional seasoning onto the freshly cut sides of the meat, then slide the foil pan into the smoker. Let the brisket cook for about 60 minutes, until the pieces darken and form a crisp crust.

**3.** Pour in half of the BBQ sauce and stir gently to coat the meat. Add more if needed, then place the tray back in the smoker and cook for another 15 to 20 minutes, until the sauce is tacky.

**4.** This recipe is all about intuition and feeling—there are no hard rules. If it looks good and feels right, it's time to serve. Sauce them up a bit more, pile the burnt ends on your choice of bun, and top with pickles and thinly sliced white onion for texture, freshness, and a bit of acidity to enhance the beefy flavors. Enjoy your pitmaster's treat!

**Note:** If you're using leftovers, follow the same steps. Allow the brisket to warm up for about 30 minutes before adding the additional seasoning. Then, continue cooking as instructed.

# SOUTHERN BRISKET SUNRISE

**MAKES 4 SANDWICHES**
**EQUIPMENT: SKILLET OR GRIDDLE**

2 tablespoons (28 g unsalted butter, divided

4 breakfast buns (see bread recommendations)

4 eggs

1 pound (454 g) Overnight Brisket point (p. 119), thickly sliced

Jalapeño Cream Cheese (p. 69)

¼ cup (80 g) peach preserves

**BREAD RECOMMENDATIONS:**

Large croissants

English muffins

Buttermilk biscuits

Glazed donuts, sliced in half and toasted (yes, really)

**Of course you can have barbecue in the morning! Toss it in a buttery croissant and it's easy to convince the skeptical crew that brisket is suddenly a proper brunch. The heat of the jalapeños cuts through the creaminess of the cream cheese, while the peach preserves bring a touch of sweetness to every bite, creating the perfect contrast. Topped with a butter-fried egg and piled into a toasted croissant, this meal is a celebration of all the hard work and flavors that went into the overnight cook.**

**1.** Split the croissants down the middle to create a sandwich base. Heat a cast-iron skillet or griddle over medium heat. Add 1 tablespoon (14 g) of butter to the pan, and once melted, place the croissants face down, gently browning them until golden. Remove from the pan when they're perfectly toasted.

**2.** Melt the remaining butter in the skillet. When it starts to foam, add the eggs. As they cook, carefully tilt the pan toward you so the butter pools. Using a spoon, baste the hot butter over the egg whites until no jiggly white remains, about 2 to 3 minutes. Remove the eggs from the pan.

**3.** Add the slices of brisket to the pan and warm them through for about 2 to 3 minutes, flipping as needed. Remove from the pan—it's time to build your breakfast.

**4.** Starting with the bottom half of the toasted croissant, smear on the Jalapeño Cream Cheese, then add a slice of warm brisket, the egg, and top with a little bit of peach preserves. This sandwich makes for a perfect brunch, followed by a much-needed nap.

5

# IS IT A SANDWICH? WRAPS, TOASTS, AND MORE

# SMOKY HOT BROWN

**MAKES 4 SANDWICHES**
**EQUIPMENT: SKILLET**

8 slices bacon

4 eggs

4 thick slices bread (see bread recommendations)

**FOR MORNAY SAUCE:**

¼ cup (56 g) butter

¼ cup (30 g) all-purpose flour

2½ cups (588 ml) warm whole milk, plus more as needed

2 ounces (57 g) freshly grated Gruyère cheese

2 ounces (57 g) freshly grated Parmesan cheese

1½ pounds (680 g) Smoked Turkey Breast (p. 78), sliced thin

Diced tomatoes

Diced parsley, celery leaves, or chives

**BREAD RECOMMENDATIONS:**

Sourdough bread

Texas toast (crust removed; it's classic)

Pullman's loaf

White bread

**I fell in love while in Kentucky, and it was with the hot brown. This classic open-faced turkey sandwich layered with bacon, tomatoes, and a velvety cheese sauce that might make you feel a little guilty. My breakfast version uses toasted sourdough to elevate the slowly smoked turkey breast, topped with bacon, egg, and a silky Mornay sauce. It's rich, decadent, and totally worth the wait—just make sure you have a comfy spot to crash afterward.**

**1.** Place a cast-iron skillet over medium heat and add the bacon strips. Cook slowly, flipping as needed, until the bacon crisps up. Once crispy, remove the bacon and set it aside to drain on a paper towel. Drop the eggs into the skillet, spooning the hot bacon fat over the egg whites until they're no longer jiggly. Cook the eggs to your preferred doneness, then remove them from the pan.

**2.** Toast the bread in the remaining bacon fat for about a minute, until golden brown. Remove the toast and set it aside.

**3.** Now, prepare the Mornay Sauce (it's best served right after it's made). In a heavy saucepan, melt butter over medium-low heat. Stir in the flour and cook for 2 to 3 minutes, whisking constantly, until the mixture becomes bubbly and until it forms a thick paste (known as a roux). Cook the roux over medium-low heat for about 2 minutes, stirring frequently. Gradually whisk in the whole milk, then cook over medium heat until the milk begins to simmer, about 2 to 3 minutes. Remove the sauce from the heat and slowly whisk in the cheeses until the Mornay sauce is smooth and creamy. Add more milk if needed. If the sauce sits too long and thickens, just heat it on low and stir to loosen it up.

**4.** Using the skillet from the bacon, gently warm the turkey slices over medium-low heat, flipping as needed until ready to serve.

**5.** Assemble the hot brown by placing the toasted bread on the bottom, followed by the turkey, bacon, and egg. Pour the warm Mornay sauce over the top and garnish with diced tomatoes and parsley, celery leaves, or chives. Serve immediately.

# CHILE RELLENO SONORAN HOT DOG

**MAKES 8 HOT DOGS**
**EQUIPMENT: GRILL**

- 8 hot dogs
- 8 Anaheim or Hatch chiles
- 2 cups (230 g) shredded Oaxaca or Monterey Jack cheese, divided
- Fresh Mayonnaise (p. 157)
- 8 split-top hot dog buns
- Guacamole Spread (p. 159)
- Sour Cream Sandwich Sauce (p. 159) or Mexican crema
- 1 cup (180 g) diced tomatoes

**Back in my twenties, I was a regular at the late-night hot dog carts in downtown Phoenix, always grabbing the local favorite: Sonoran Dogs. These come loaded with toppings like mayo, ketchup, bacon, pickled jalapenos, guacamole, and just about anything else you can think of. No matter what was on top, every single bite seemed to satisfy whatever craving you had at the time. My version takes that Sonoran Dog and kicks it up a notch by stuffing a smoked hot dog and cheese into a chile relleno. It's a perfect, buttery, rich bite followed by all the zingy toppings you crave.**

**1.** Preheat the grill for two-zone cooking by banking the coals to one side, aiming for a temperature around 400°F (204°C). Add wood chips or chunks for extra flavor. Place the hot dogs on the cool side of the grill and the chiles over the coals. Flip the peppers occasionally, grilling until the skin is charred on all sides and they've softened. Remove the peppers and place them in a sealed container or resealable bag to steam for about 6 to 8 minutes. Close the lid of the grill to let the hot dogs smoke.

**2.** Once the peppers have cooled, carefully remove the skins. Use a sharp knife to make a slit along one side of each pepper and remove the seeds and stem. Fill each pepper with ¼ cup (28 g) of the shredded cheese.

**3.** Once the hot dogs are cooked to your preferred doneness, carefully place each one while still warm into a cheese-stuffed pepper. Spread a little mayo on each bun, then add the stuffed peppers to the buns. Transfer the buns to the cool side of the grill and close the lid for a couple of minutes to melt the cheese.

**4.** Top the warm hot dogs with guacamole, sour cream sauce or crema, and tomatoes. Enjoy a taste of Arizona—and make sure you've got a cold brew handy, because trust me, you'll be going back for seconds (or thirds).

# CHEESE-STUFFED CHORIPÁN

**SERVES ABOUT 4**
**EQUIPMENT: CHARCOAL GRILL**

Chimichurri (p. 91)

2 sandwich rolls, about 12 to 14 inches (30 to 36 cm) long (see bread recommendations)

1 pound (454 g) provolone or mozzarella cheese, thickly sliced

2 pounds (907 g) Argentinian chorizo or Italian sausages, raw in casing

2 large tomatoes, sliced

Kosher salt and coarsely ground black pepper to taste

**BREAD RECOMMENDATIONS:**

French rolls

Italian rolls

Soft baguettes

**Choripán is an iconic Argentinian classic that celebrates the simple yet perfect combination of bread, meat, and cheese. This version takes it up a notch with melty cheese stuffed into a trench in the crusty bread, hiding underneath a thin layer of chorizo. Layering them together and searing on the grill turns simple ingredients into something next-level. It's one of the easiest and most delicious almost-sandwiches I've ever had. Place some fresh tomatoes and chimichurri on top, and that's all you need to make your day complete.**

**1.** Make the Chimichurri.

**2.** Slice the sandwich rolls into top and bottom halves and hollow out a trench in each half. Tear the cheese and place it into the trench, filling up each slice.

**3.** Remove the chorizo or sausage from the casings and form thin patties, pressing them firmly onto the bread halves on top of the cheese. Make sure the layer is even and goes all the way to the edges of the bread.

**4.** Preheat the grill for two-zone cooking by banking the coals to one side, aiming for a temperature around 400°F (204°C). Place the rolls, sausage side-down, on the hot side of the grill. Grill for about 4 to 5 minutes, or until char marks form. Rotate the meat as needed to evenly sear, then flip and move to the cooler side of the grill. Close the lid and cook for another 5 to 6 minutes or until the internal temperature reaches 155°F (68°C).

**5.** Serve immediately, topping with fresh slices of tomato, salt and pepper, and plenty of chimichurri. Slice the bread into pieces and serve.

# YEMENI LAMB PITA WITH ZHUG

**SERVES ABOUT 8 TO 12**
**EQUIPMENT: SMOKER**

1 bone-in lamb shoulder, 5 to 8 pounds (2.3 to 3.6 kg)

½ cup (100 g) Prime Smoke Rub (p. 173)

1 tablespoon (6 g) ground coriander

½ tablespoon (4 g) ground turmeric

1 teaspoon ground cumin

½ teaspoon ground cinnamon

½ teaspoon ground clove

**FOR ZHUG SAUCE:**

12 to 16 serrano chiles, stems removed, roughly chopped

4 garlic cloves, roughly chopped

2 tablespoons (30 ml) lemon juice, plus more as needed

1 cup (60 g) parsley

1 cup (16 g) cilantro

1 tablespoon (6 g) ground coriander

1 tablespoon (7 g) ground cardamom

1 tablespoon (18 g) kosher salt, plus more as needed

¾ cup (177 ml) olive oil

**FOR TAHINI SAUCE:**

½ cup (120 g) tahini

1 garlic clove, grated

½ teaspoon sea salt

¼ cup (59 ml) freshly squeezed lemon juice

6 tablespoons (89 ml) water, plus more as needed

4 to 6 fresh baked pitas

Lettuce, shredded

Cucumbers, sliced thin

Tomato, sliced

Red onion, sliced thin

**When it comes to sandwiches (okay, maybe it's technically a pita, but who's counting?), this one knocks it out of the park. Smoked lamb shoulder, seasoned with warm spices and slow cooked to tender perfection, gets stuffed into freshly baked pitas. A creamy tahini sauce smooths out the heat from the fiery zhug, creating the perfect balance. Every bite is a contrast of flavors—crisp veggies, smoky lamb, and that sharp chile kick that bounces the tastebuds all over. This is one of my favorite bites in the cookbook, so don't skip it.**

**1.** Prepare the smoker for cooking at 250°F (121°C), using a mild wood like apple, pecan, or oak to complement the lamb. Pat the lamb shoulder dry with paper towels, then combine the rub with the coriander, turmeric, cumin, cinnamon, and clove in a small bowl. Season the lamb generously on all sides and let it rest at room temperature while the smoker warms up.

**2.** Place the seasoned lamb shoulder fat-side up into the warm smoker and let it cook undisturbed for about 4 hours.

CONTINUED →

## YEMENI LAMB PITA WITH ZHUG, CONTINUED

**3.** While the lamb is smoking, make the Zhug Sauce. Add the chopped chiles, garlic, and lemon juice to a food processor, pulsing a few times to finely mince the ingredients. Scrape down the sides as needed. Add the parsley, cilantro, coriander, cardamom, and salt. Puree until almost smooth. With the motor running on low, slowly drizzle in the olive oil to form a thicker paste. Taste and adjust with more salt or lemon juice if needed.

**4.** Combine the ingredients for the Tahini Sauce, adding more water as needed to thin it out. If the sauce is too thick or clumpy, just add a little more water and stir until smooth.

**5.** Check the lamb with an internal meat thermometer. The target temperature should be around 200°F to 205°F (93°C to 96°C), and the meat should feel probe-tender, indicating it's ready for shredding. Depending on the size of your lamb and its fat content, cooking time may vary, and it could take additional time. Once it reaches the target temperature and feels tender, remove the lamb shoulder from the smoker and double-wrap it in heavy-duty aluminum foil. Let it rest for about 35 to 45 minutes.

**6.** After resting is complete, remove the lamb from the foil and discard the bones. Wearing gloves, shred the meat. Warm the pitas and split them open, then fill them with shredded lettuce, cucumbers, tomatoes, onions, and smoked lamb. Serve with a side of Tahini Sauce and Zhug Sauce. Be careful—the zhug packs a punch of heat!

**Note:** If you have a mortar and pestle (or molcajete), use it to prepare the Zhug Sauce by grinding the chiles, herbs, and spices before slowly adding the oil to emulsify the sauce. The texture will be creamier and the flavor richer than when using a food processor.

# SMASH BURGER TACOS

**MAKES 8 TACOS**
**EQUIPMENT: GRIDDLE**

---

**FOR BURGER SAUCE:**

½ cup (115 g) Fresh Mayonnaise (p. 157)

¼ cup (60 g) ketchup

½ teaspoon paprika

½ teaspoon onion powder

½ teaspoon garlic powder

2 teaspoons pickle juice

Salt and coarsely ground black pepper to taste

1½ pounds (680 g) ground beef, 80/20

8 small flour tortillas

Salt and coarsely ground black pepper to taste

1 tablespoon (15 ml) avocado oil

8 slices American cheese

1 cup (135 g) chopped Fresh Pickles (p. 178) or Quick Pickles (p. 181)

1 cup (160 g) finely diced white onion

2 cups (110 g) shredded lettuce

Toasted sesame seeds

**This recipe went viral for a reason: crispy beef, melty cheese, and all your favorite burger toppings come together in a toasty flour tortilla for the ultimate loaded bite. If you're a burger fan, this recipe delivers all the flavors you love, packed into a handy, taco-sized package. They cook surprisingly fast, so dinner's ready in no time.**

**1.** Start by mixing up the Burger Sauce. Taste it and adjust with salt and pepper to your liking. Set it aside in the fridge until you're ready to use it.

**2.** Next, prepare your meat. Shape the beef into 8 evenly sized portions, about the size of a golf ball. Lay a flour tortilla down, then press a ball of meat onto it using wax paper and a small baking sheet to smash it flat. The patty should nearly reach the edge of the tortilla. Do this for the rest of the tacos, and season with salt and pepper to taste. This pre-smashing trick is perfect if you're making a larger batch. Of course, if you prefer, you can always smash the meat directly on the hot griddle using a burger press and the tortilla.

**3.** Wipe the oil onto the griddle and turn it on to a medium-high heat for searing. Turn on only half of the burners for cooking, and use the other half to keep your tacos warm as you prepare the rest. This also helps gently warm the backs of the tacos, ensuring the meat cooks all the way through.

**4.** Place the tortillas meat-side down on the hot griddle, pressing with your spatula to smash them into the surface. Do this for all of the tortillas, allowing them to sear for about 3 to 4 minutes. Check the edges; the burger should be cooked about 80 to 90 percent through with a crispy brown edge. Using your spatula, scrape the burger from the griddle and flip to the cooler side, which should have some ambient heat. Add the slices of cheese and continue cooking the rest of the burgers.

**5.** Take the tacos off when ready and top with chopped pickles, onions, the Burger Sauce, lettuce, and toasted sesame seeds. You'll be surprised at how fast they disappear!

# Taco 'Bout a Smash Hit: Going Global

**I WOKE UP ON A MONDAY,** a few days after I shared my smash burger taco recipe on Instagram for the first time. I couldn't believe my inbox—*The Washington Post,* Today.com, Yahoo News, ABC—it was flooded with inquiries about my story and how I came up with this recipe.

The funny thing is, it wasn't some grand plan. It was just a solution. On Mondays, I'd make simple, delicious smash burgers for my kids after school. One week, I forgot to buy buns and didn't realize it until dinner time. Living in Arizona, we always have tortillas in the house, so I figured I'd give that a try. The kids might think it was silly, but I was sure they'd eat it.

I threw the beef balls onto the hot griddle, slapped a flour tortilla on top, and pressed it down with my burger press. Sure enough, the meat stuck to the tortilla. I wasn't sure it was going to cook all the way through, but the meat was thin, so I wasn't worried. The steam created a sticky bond, helping the meat attach to the tortilla without sliding off.

I flipped the burger with my spatula, and that was it: proof of concept. It might not have been some genius breakthrough, but it was pretty exciting and fun. I topped it with American cheese and my usual toppings and served it to the family. It's amazing how much more a burger tastes like a burger when you eat it this way, it's just an explosion of beef, cheese, and crispy toppings all at once. It's almost overwhelming at first, but then you go for a second one.

In the days that followed, I received tons of emails and DMs, people tagging me in recipes and sharing their own versions. Everyone started remaking it online, even remixing it with different meats and toppings. My recipe had over 200 million views across my platforms within a week—even Gordon Ramsay and Chrissy Teigen made it!

I'm humbled by how something so simple, made in our little backyard, could have such a big impact. I hope you enjoy smash burger tacos as much as we do, along with the other tasty creations in this book!

# MARGARITA SHRIMP AVOCADO TOAST

**MAKES 4 TO 5 TOASTS**
**EQUIPMENT: GRILL**

- 1 pound (454 g) shrimp, peeled and deveined
- 3 tablespoons (44 ml) avocado oil
- 3 tablespoons (3 g) chopped fresh cilantro
- 2 tablespoons (30 ml) fresh lime juice
- 2 cloves garlic, minced
- 2 teaspoons tequila
- 1 jalapeño, diced
- ¼ teaspoon kosher salt, plus more to taste
- 4 bamboo skewers, soaked in water for 20 minutes
- 2 avocados

- Softened butter, for toasting
- 4 to 5 slices bread (see bread recommendations)
- Juice of 2 limes
- ½ cup (8 g) chopped cilantro
- 1 cup (135 g) finely diced English cucumber
- Red onion, thinly sliced, or Pickled Red Onions (p. 183)
- Lime wedges to garnish

**BREAD RECOMMENDATIONS:**
- Whole-grain bread
- Seeded sliced bread
- Sourdough
- Country loaf
- Levain bread

**Don't roll your eyes, this is avocado toast worth making because it's loaded with grilled shrimp. I can't help but think of vacation time when I'm eating avocados, so I wanted to bring that vibe to the recipe. Margarita flavors, including tequila, make a zesty marinade for the shrimp, which tastes even better seared over the fire. Piled on top of grilled avocados, crisp cucumbers, and sharp onions, this will completely change the way you enjoy your avocado toast. So raise those pinkies, click those tongs, and let's dig in.**

**1.** Mix the shrimp, oil, cilantro, lime juice, garlic, tequila, jalapeños, and salt in a bowl. Cover the bowl with plastic wrap and let the shrimp marinate in the fridge for about 30 minutes.

**2.** While the shrimp marinates, soak your wooden skewers in warm water (skip this step if using metal skewers).

**3.** Preheat the grill for direct cooking over medium heat, around 300°F to 350°F (149°C to 177°C). Clean the grates well so the shrimp don't stick. Remove the shrimp from the marinade and thread them onto the skewers, piercing each shrimp twice to secure them.

**4.** Place the skewers on the grill directly over the coals and grill for 2 to 3 minutes. Flip and grill the other side for another 2 to 3 minutes, then flip once more until the shrimp reach an internal temperature of about 120°F (49°C). The shrimp should be opaque and firm to the touch when done.

**5.** While the shrimp cooks, halve the avocados and remove the pits. Place the avocado halves on the grill, face down, for 3 to 4 minutes until they have nice grill marks. Remove them from the grill and set aside. Butter the bread and toast it on the grill for a couple of minutes until golden brown.

**6.** Remove the skins from the grilled avocados. Mash the avocados with the juice of 2 limes and salt, then spread the mixture onto the toasted bread. Top with the grilled shrimp, cilantro, diced cucumber, and red onions. Add a sprinkle of salt to taste, and serve with lime wedges on the side.

# GRILLED CHICKEN STACK

**MAKES 4 SANDWICHES**
**EQUIPMENT: CHARCOAL GRILL**

- 8 boneless and skinless chicken breast fillets, 6 to 8 ounces (170 to 227 g) each
- 1½ cups (355 ml) milk
- ½ cup (118 ml) pickle juice
- 3 tablespoons (44 ml) avocado oil
- ½ cup (111 g) Sweet Smolder Rub (p. 174), plus more as needed
- 4 slices pepper jack cheese

**FOR CHICKEN SAUCE:**

- ½ cup (115 g) Fresh Mayonnaise (p. 157)
- 1 tablespoon (15 ml) hot sauce
- 2 teaspoons yellow mustard
- ½ teaspoon paprika
- ½ teaspoon onion powder
- ¼ teaspoon fine sea salt
- ¼ teaspoon garlic powder

- 8 pieces thick-cut bacon, cooked
- Fresh Pickles (p. 178) or Quick Pickles (p. 181)

**Years ago, a fast-food chain came up with a wild idea: a chicken sandwich with two pieces of fried chicken as the "bread." Yup, I tried it—and yeah, it was surprisingly delicious. Even though it was a little over the top, I've always wondered, *Could I make this at home? How could I make it better?* Well, this might not be fried chicken, but it's juicy and tender smoked chicken breast with a hint of smoke and fire. Pair it with a tangy sauce, crispy bacon, and pickles, and suddenly, you might not even miss the buns. Oh, and gluten-free folks, this one's for you too.**

**1.** Grab a large resealable bag and lay the chicken flat inside—this will become your marinade bag. Take a skillet or a heavy pan and gently smack them into an even thickness, roughly ½-inch (1-cm) thick—this helps them cook evenly on the grill. If your chicken breasts are super thick, no need to smack—just slice them in half lengthwise to create thinner fillets. For smaller breasts, butterflying them works just as well.

**2.** Pour the milk and pickle juice into the bag with the chicken. Gently massage the bag to mix everything together. Squeeze out as much air as possible and seal it up, letting the chicken marinate for about 45 minutes. The milk and pickle juice combo will tenderize the chicken and keep it juicy.

**3.** Meanwhile, make the sauce by combining the ingredients in a small bowl. Then, cook the bacon—my go-to method is in the oven at 400°F (204°C) for 20 minutes on a baking sheet, flipping halfway through. Drain the bacon on paper towels and set aside.

**4.** Once the chicken is marinated, remove and pat the chicken dry. Lightly oil each chicken breast, then season generously with the sweet rub. Let the chicken rest while you prep the grill.

**CONTINUED →**

## GRILLED CHICKEN STACK, CONTINUED

**5.** Preheat the grill for two-zone cooking by banking the coals to one side, aiming for a temperature around 400°F (204°C). Clean the grates. Remove the chicken from the marinade and place it directly over the coals to sear. After about 2 to 3 minutes, flip the chicken—it should release easily from the grates—and sear the other side for another 2 to 3 minutes. Move the chicken to the cooler side of the grill, close the lid, and leave the vents slightly open for indirect cooking. Let the chicken cook for another 15 to 20 minutes, or until it reaches 160°F to 162°F (71°C to 72°C).

**6.** Remove the chicken and lay slices of cheese on half of the breasts while they're still warm. Tent loosely with foil and let them rest for a few minutes.

**7.** Assemble the "sandwich" with a cheesy chicken breast on the bottom, followed by 2 pieces (or more!) of bacon, pickles, sauce, and the top "bun"—which is, of course, another chicken breast.

# 6

# LAYERING FLAVORS: BREADS, SAUCES, AND CONDIMENTS

# BREADS: EVERY SANDWICH'S FOUNDATION

**YOU MIGHT BE SURPRISED TO LEARN** that there are no bread recipes in this book. I can't pretend to be a baking guru. Spoiler alert: I'm not. But I do believe that fresh, thoughtfully chosen bread is the real hero of any sandwich (dad joke, gotcha!).

Choosing the right bread is like picking the right BBQ sauce for your meat. It's all about balance and bringing everything together. You could have the juiciest, smokiest pulled pork or the crispiest bacon, but if that bread can't hold its own, your sandwich will flop harder than a soggy bun at the bottom of a pool. The bread isn't just the foundation; it's the unsung hero, working to elevate all those juicy, crispy fillings into something magical.

Texture matters here. I can't emphasize that enough. The bread is the first thing that greets your mouth—its crunch, softness, and chewiness are all part of the initial experience. Maybe you're craving that crispy, golden brown crust that delivers a satisfying crackle, creating that delightful contrast when you bite into the sandwich. But maybe that's not your thing. Maybe you're into something softer, with a pillowy center that melts in your mouth as you bite into those hearty textures. Choices matter. *It's all about what you want that sandwich to do for you.* Does it need to support a loaded burger? Or should it soak up the last bit of spicy mop sauce like a pro? The right bread makes all those things possible.

While some of us may have mastered the art of the perfectly grilled steak, not all of us are whipping up sourdough from scratch (raises hand here). If you love baking bread at home, I sincerely applaud you. It's a skill I haven't quite mastered, and the world definitely needs more people like you.

But here's something I *can* do: Support local bakeries. And that's where the magic happens. Supporting your local bakeries isn't just about keeping your community thriving; it's about getting top-notch bread that knows exactly what it's doing when it comes to creating the perfect sandwich canvas. If you're serious about your sandwich game, you've got to check out the local spots.

Don't just limit yourself to the typical deli-style bread either. Try something new and exciting—maybe a hearty, rustic loaf from a nearby bakery that's been around for generations. Or take a trip to that Middle Eastern bakery down the street,

**Note:** Speaking of local spots, I want to take a moment to highlight and thank Noble Bread, located here in Phoenix. They've supplied countless loaves of bread and generously shared their time to support the cookbook, while also educating me throughout my research.

where you'll find soft, pillowy pita or fresh, sesame-studded flatbreads that could elevate a simple sandwich into something extraordinary. These bakeries often craft breads with a distinct character you can't get anywhere else. You'll enjoy a fresh, unique taste that you won't find at a chain store—and you'll be supporting a local business in the process.

When you explore local bakeries, you're not just picking up bread; you're uncovering a world of flavors and textures. From the delicate sweetness of challah to the chewy, dense pull of ciabatta, there's an entire spectrum of options to try. Who knows? You might discover a new favorite bread to pair with smoky brisket or spicy pulled pork. Trust me, it'll be worth the trip—and it'll make your sandwiches taste even better.

If you're like me and would rather spend your free time smoking meats than baking, take a moment to visit your local bakeries next time you need bread. No matter where you live, there's a bakery ready to help you take your sandwiches to the next level.

# FRESH MAYONNAISE

**MAKES ABOUT 2 CUPS (450 G)**

- 2 large eggs
- 2 tablespoons (22 g) Dijon mustard
- 2 tablespoons (30 ml) fresh lemon juice or vinegar of choice, plus more as needed
- Kosher salt to taste
- 2 cups (473 ml) neutral oil, such as avocado, sunflower, or grapeseed

**The cornerstone condiment for sandwiches has to be mayonnaise. If you haven't made it from scratch yet, you're in for a treat. Homemade mayo levels up the flavor and texture, and it only takes a few minutes to make. You're in control of the ingredients, from the eggs and oil to the mustard and vinegar. The best part? Unlimited flavor combinations and mix-ins. Check out some of the suggestions below. Fresh mayo will last about 10 to 14 days in the fridge, but if you're making sandwiches regularly, that shouldn't be a problem.**

### USING A FOOD PROCESSOR

**1.** Add the eggs to a small food processor bowl and process for 15 seconds. Add the mustard, lemon juice or vinegar, and salt to taste, and process for another 15 seconds until the mixture is smooth.

**2.** Scrape the sides of the bowl, turn the processor on, and slowly add the oil a few drops at a time until about a quarter of it is incorporated (this helps with emulsification). Once the mixture begins to thicken, you can add the rest of the oil in a thin stream instead of drops.

**3.** After all the oil is added, scrape the sides again and process for 10 more seconds. Taste and adjust with salt and lemon juice or vinegar as needed.

### USING AN IMMERSION BLENDER

**1.** Add all of your mayonnaise ingredients (including the oil) to a tall, narrow mason jar. Place the blender at the bottom of the jar and turn it on. Slowly pull the blender up through the middle of the jar to blend in the oil, then push it back down and around to mix everything together. Repeat this a couple of times until the mayo thickens up.

**2.** Taste and adjust with extra salt or lemon juice as needed.

CONTINUED →

# FRESH MAYONNAISE, CONTINUED

## More Flavors

**Chipotle Mayonnaise:** Process or blend 1 cup (225 g) Fresh Mayonnaise, 2 chipotles in adobo sauce, and 1 tablespoon (15 ml) fresh lime juice.

**Horseradish Mayonnaise:** Mix 1 cup (225 g) Fresh Mayonnaise, 2 tablespoons (30 g) prepared horseradish, 2 tablespoons (6 g) fresh chives or parsley, and 1 tablespoon (15 ml) fresh lemon juice.

**Dijonnaise:** Mix 1 cup (225 g) Fresh Mayonnaise, 3 tablespoons (33 g) Dijon mustard, 2 tablespoons (30 g) prepared horseradish, and 1 tablespoon (15 ml) fresh lemon juice.

**Cilantro Mayonnaise:** Process or blend 1 cup (225 g) Fresh Mayonnaise, ½ cup (8 g) packed fresh cilantro (stems included), and 2 tablespoons (30 ml) fresh lime juice.

**Korean Mayonnaise:** Mix ¼ cup (60 g) Fresh Mayonnaise or Kewpie mayo, 2 tablespoons (30 g) gochujang, and 2 to 3 tablespoons (30 to 44 ml) kimchi brine.

**Sriracha Mayonnaise:** Mix 1 cup (225 g) Fresh Mayonnaise and 2 tablespoons (30 ml) sriracha hot sauce.

**Jalapeño Mayonnaise:** Mix 1 cup (225 g) Fresh Mayonnaise, 1 minced jalapeño pepper, ½ teaspoon garlic powder, and 2 tablespoons (30 ml) fresh lime juice.

**Charred Scallion Aioli:** Process or blend 1 cup (225 g) Fresh Mayonnaise, 1 bunch of grilled scallions (p. 70), 1 grated garlic clove, and juice of 1 lemon.

**Black Garlic Mayonnaise:** Mix 1 cup (225 g) Fresh Mayonnaise and 3 cloves (about 1 tablespoon [6 g]) black garlic.

# SOUR CREAM SANDWICH SAUCE

**MAKES ABOUT 1½ CUPS (340 G)**

- 1 cup (230 g) sour cream
- ¼ cup (60 g) Fresh Mayonnaise (p. 157)
- 2 tablespoons (30 ml) freshly squeezed lime juice, plus more as needed
- ½ teaspoon ground cumin
- ½ teaspoon cayenne pepper, plus more as needed
- Salt to taste

**This tangy sauce is perfect for sandwiches that need a little extra zing. It's not too much mayo, not too much sour cream—just the perfect balance between both worlds. Try it on anything with Southwest or Mexican flavors, like the Fajita Smash Burgers (p. 27) or the Carnitas Torta (p. 109).**

**1.** Add the ingredients to a food processor and mix until smooth. Taste and adjust with salt, cayenne, and lime juice. Store in the fridge; it will be fresh for 5 to 7 days.

# GUACAMOLE SPREAD

**MAKES ABOUT 2 CUPS (450 G)**

- 2 Hass avocados, ripe but not mushy
- 1 tablespoon (15 ml) freshly squeezed lime juice
- 1 tablespoon (15 ml) olive oil
- ½ teaspoon garlic powder
- ¼ teaspoon coarsely ground black pepper
- Kosher salt to taste

**Sure, you can make a big batch of fresh guac (good luck not eating it first), but this smooth spread is perfect for sandwiches. It gets into all those little nooks and crannies of the bread, delivering that burst of rich freshness to balance out the barbecue. Storing it in a squeeze bottle or jar in the fridge will keep it bright green for days. Add some cilantro if you want an extra herby punch.**

**1.** Add the ingredients to a food processor and mix until smooth. Taste and adjust with salt and lime juice. Store in the fridge; it will be fresh for 5 to 7 days.

# BUFFALO BBQ SAUCE

**MAKES ABOUT 2¾ CUPS (660 G)**

- 1 cup (267 ml) cayenne hot sauce, such as Frank's RedHot
- 1 cup (240 g) ketchup
- ¼ cup (60 g) brown sugar
- 2 tablespoons (40 g) molasses
- ¼ cup (59 ml) apple cider vinegar
- 2 teaspoons Worcestershire sauce
- 1 teaspoon chipotle powder
- 1 teaspoon coarsely ground black pepper
- 1 teaspoon celery salt
- 2 tablespoons (28 g) cold unsalted butter, cubed

**Why choose between buffalo and BBQ when you can have both? This sauce brings together the classic heat of cayenne hot sauce with a sweet, smoky barbecue twist to balance it out. Finish it off with a whisk of cold butter for that velvety richness you expect from a great buffalo sauce.**

**1.** Add all ingredients (except the butter) to a medium saucepan and cook over low heat until the sauce begins to simmer. Stir gently with a whisk to help melt the sugars and spices together. After about 8 to 10 minutes of simmering, the sauce will thicken.

**2.** Turn off the heat and whisk in the butter gradually, melting it slowly while stirring. This helps the butter emulsify into the sauce, ensuring it doesn't separate.

House
Buffalo
Chipotle

# HOUSE BBQ SAUCE

**MAKES ABOUT 2¾ CUPS (660 G)**

---

- 1 cup (240 g) ketchup
- ¼ cup (59 ml) cider vinegar
- ¼ cup (80 g) maple syrup
- ¼ cup (44 g) yellow mustard
- ¼ cup (85 g) molasses
- ¼ cup (80 g) peach preserves
- 2 tablespoons (30 ml) water
- 1 tablespoon (15 ml) Worcestershire sauce
- 1 teaspoon onion powder
- 1 tablespoon (9 g) garlic powder
- 1 tablespoon (2 g) coarsely ground black pepper
- 1 teaspoon ground cumin
- 1 teaspoon ground coriander
- ½ teaspoon kosher salt, plus more as needed

**This bottle of sauce is a staple in our house, always ready to take any meal to the next level. The flavor profile isn't tied to any specific region of barbecue; it's just plain delicious. While it starts with a ketchup base, the mustard and cider vinegar give it a tangy edge, and the maple syrup, peaches, and molasses add layers of sweetness that make it truly special. Pair it with anything smoked—chicken, pork, shrimp, or yes, even brisket (I said it). It's perfect with burnt ends, and we've even been known to drizzle it on a brisket taco when we're feeling fancy.**

**1.** Combine the ingredients in a saucepan and bring to a low boil over medium heat, stirring to mix everything together. Reduce the heat to low and let the sauce simmer for 5 to 6 minutes. Use an immersion blender to blitz the sauce (or carefully pour it into a blender) before straining it through a fine sieve.

**2.** Once cool, store in an airtight glass jar. This sauce will stay fresh for about 10 to 14 days.

# CHIPOTLE BBQ SAUCE

**MAKES ABOUT 2½ CUPS (600 G)**

- 1 cup (240 g) ketchup
- ½ cup (115 g) brown sugar
- ½ cup (170 g) honey
- ¼ cup (36 g) chipotles in adobo sauce
- 3 teaspoons (44 ml) apple cider vinegar
- 2 teaspoons Worcestershire sauce
- 2 tablespoons (30 ml) water
- 1 teaspoon garlic powder
- 1 teaspoon coarsely ground black pepper
- ½ teaspoon) kosher salt, more to taste

**If there's one chili pepper that belongs with barbecue, it's the smoky, fruity chipotle. This spicy sauce uses just a few ingredients, letting the sweetness from honey and brown sugar balance out the tang. Want more heat? Just add more chipotles!**

**1.** Combine the ingredients in a saucepan and bring to a low boil over medium heat, stirring to mix everything together. Reduce the heat to low and let the sauce simmer for 5 to 6 minutes. Use an immersion blender to blitz the sauce (or carefully pour it into a blender) before straining it through a fine sieve.

**2.** Once cool, store in an airtight glass jar. This sauce will stay fresh for about 10 to 14 days.

# CREAMY CHEESE SAUCE

**MAKES ABOUT 3 CUPS (710 G)**

- 8 ounces (227 g) (about 2 cups) freshly shredded cheddar cheese
- 4 ounces (113 g) (about 1 cup) freshly shredded pepper jack cheese
- 1½ tablespoons (12 g) cornstarch
- 1 can (12-ounce [355 g]) evaporated milk, plus more as needed
- 2 teaspoons hot sauce or pickled jalapeño juice

**Sometimes you just need a quick cheese sauce that melts over everything. This is a very simple, customizable sauce you can whip up in a few minutes. Swap out the cheeses or flavors of hot sauce and find the combo that works for you. It's amazing on the Pit Beef 'N' Cheddar (p. 25) or the kicked-up Smoky Cheesy Joe (p. 16).**

**1.** Combine the cheese and cornstarch. Toss them together to coat, and add them to a medium, heavy-bottomed saucepan over low heat.

**2.** Add the evaporated milk and hot sauce, then whisk continuously until the cheese melts. Keep whisking for about 5 minutes until it's bubbly and thickened to your liking.

**3.** If it thickens too much, just add a little more milk to get it where you want.

**4.** Serve it up right away and watch it vanish. It's best enjoyed fresh and hot—once it cools, the texture just isn't the same. Keep it at a very low heat until it's time to eat.

# CRISPY SANDWICH SLAW

**MAKES ABOUT 12 SERVINGS**

- ½ head green cabbage, finely shredded on a mandolin or by hand
- ½ head red cabbage, finely shredded on a mandolin or by hand
- 1 large red onion, finely sliced on a mandolin or by hand
- 1 large carrot, peeled and grated on the large holes of a box grater
- 2 jalapeños, thinly sliced into rings, optional
- ½ cup (100 g) white sugar
- ½ cup (150 g) kosher salt, plus more as needed

- ¾ cup (175 g) Fresh Mayonnaise (p. 157)
- ¼ cup (59 ml) apple cider vinegar
- 2 tablespoons (22 g) Dijon mustard
- 1 tablespoon (6 g) freshly ground black pepper
- 1 tablespoon (15 ml) hot sauce, plus more as needed
- ¼ cup (15 g) roughly chopped fresh parsley or cilantro leaves

**I've been making my own versions of slaw for over a decade, ever since I read about how chef J. Kenji López-Alt cures cabbage with salt and sugar to draw out the moisture and deeply season the veggies. This version is inspired by his method, but I've thrown in a little extra heat and crunch for good measure. It's the perfect topper for most sandwiches, and let me tell you—it's especially killer with pulled pork, pulled chicken, or smoked turkey. (Just try it on the Smokin' Hot Rachel—page 87—and thank me later.)**

**1.** Combine shredded cabbages, sliced onion, grated carrots, jalapeños (if using), sugar, and salt in a large bowl, tossing to coat. Let it rest for 5 minutes, then transfer it to a colander or strainer and rinse thoroughly under cold running water. Dry the cabbage mix with a salad spinner, or layer it between paper towels on a baking sheet to blot dry.

**2.** To prepare the dressing, combine the rest of the ingredients, except the chopped herbs, in a medium bowl and whisk until everything is combined. Stir in the herbs, taste, and season with salt or additional hot sauce.

**3.** Return the shredded ingredients to the large bowl and add some of the dressing, tossing to coat. Add as much as you like, depending on how wet you prefer your slaw. Taste and adjust with more vinegar, hot sauce, salt, or sugar if desired. Store in the fridge until ready to serve. It will stay fresh for about 3 to 5 days.

# HORSERADISH SLAW

**MAKES ABOUT 12 SERVINGS**

- 1 head green cabbage, finely shredded on a mandolin or by hand
- 1 white onion, finely sliced on a mandolin or by hand
- ½ cup (100 g) plus 1 tablespoon (13 g) white sugar
- ½ cup (150 g) kosher salt, plus more as needed

- 1 cup (225 g) Fresh Mayonnaise (p. 157)
- ½ cup (115 g) sour cream
- Juice of 1 lemon
- Zest of 1 lemon
- 2 tablespoons (30 g) prepared horseradish, plus more as needed
- 1 tablespoon (11 g) Dijon mustard
- 1 teaspoon Worcestershire sauce
- ½ teaspoon celery seeds
- Freshly ground black pepper to taste

**I first started using this recipe to pair with grilled beef sandwiches, but quickly realized it works with so many other meats—smoked or grilled fish, chicken, and even shrimp. The dressing is where it shines, coating the crisp vegetables with a punch of horseradish and lemon. It's a vibrant, spicy flavor profile that's easy to customize. Toss in fresh herbs like dill, parsley, or basil for extra flavor. Want more heat? Add some cayenne hot sauce. Craving crunch? Chop up some pickles and mix them in. There's no wrong way to make this slaw your own.**

**1.** Combine shredded cabbage, sliced onion, ½ cup (100 g) of the sugar, and salt in a large bowl, tossing to coat. Let it rest for 5 minutes, then transfer it to a colander or strainer and rinse thoroughly under cold running water. Dry the cabbage mix with a salad spinner, or layer it between paper towels on a baking sheet to blot dry.

**2.** To prepare the dressing, combine the mayonnaise, sour cream, lemon juice and zest, horseradish, Dijon, Worcestershire, celery seeds, and the remaining white sugar in a medium bowl. Whisk until everything is combined. Taste and adjust with salt and pepper, or more horseradish if you want a bigger kick.

**3.** Return the shredded ingredients to the large bowl and add some of the dressing, tossing to coat. Add as much dressing as you like, depending on how wet you prefer your slaw. Taste and adjust as needed; the flavors will continue to develop as it rests. Store in the fridge until ready to serve—it will stay fresh for about 3 to 5 days.

**Note:** It may seem strange to mix the salt and sugar with the cabbage and then rinse it off, but this process removes extra water from the cabbage and also flavors it, setting the stage for delicious slaw.

# HOT HONEY

**MAKES ABOUT 1 CUP (340 G)**

- 8 to 12 dried chiles de arbol (depending on preferred heat) or 2 to 3 teaspoons (2 to 4 g) dried chili flakes
- 1 cup (340 g) honey
- 2 teaspoons apple cider vinegar

**Making your own hot honey is super simple and much more affordable than buying it premade. Plus, you get to control exactly how spicy it is! Use it in any recipe that calls for honey to add an extra kick. Stir it into mayo, ranch, or yogurt for a spicy twist on your sauces. Brush it over grilled shrimp, pork, or chicken (Honey Pepper Pimento Chicken, anyone? p. 35). This versatile condiment is a must-have in our pantry, and it'll quickly become one in yours too.**

**1.** Gently wash the chiles to remove any dust or dirt, then pat them dry. Remove the stems and chop them up, keeping the seeds.

**2.** Warm the honey over medium-low heat in a small saucepan. Add the chopped chiles to the pan. Heat until the honey just begins to simmer, around 140°F to 150°F (60°C to 66°C). Let it simmer for 1 to 2 minutes, then remove from the heat. Stir in the vinegar and let the honey infuse for 15 minutes.

**3.** Transfer the honey to a glass container. You can strain out the chiles, but leaving them in will make the honey spicier over time.

**4.** Store the honey at room temperature, sealing the jar once it's completely cooled. Avoid storing it in the fridge, as the moisture can cause it to crystallize faster.

# PRIME SMOKE RUB

**MAKES ABOUT 2½ CUPS (475 G)**

- 1 cup (300 g) kosher salt
- 1 cup (96 g) coarsely ground black pepper
- ¼ cup (36 g) granulated garlic
- 2 tablespoons (14 g) granulated onion
- 2 tablespoons (14 g) paprika
- 2 tablespoons (15 g) ancho chile powder

**This seasoning blend is perfect for both smoking and grilling, and it's a foundational recipe used throughout the book. It's based on my Canyon Crust Beef Seasoning (sold in stores), but simplified to give you the flexibility to adjust as needed. Add brown sugar for a touch of sweetness, more chile for extra heat, or even some celery salt or black pepper, depending on the meat and flavor profile you're going for. If you're planning to smoke larger cuts like pork shoulder or brisket, I highly recommend doubling this batch to make sure you have plenty to work with.**

**1.** Combine the ingredients in a medium bowl and store in an airtight container in a cool, dark place. For best freshness, use within 4 to 6 months.

# SWEET SMOLDER RUB

**MAKES ABOUT 4 CUPS (800 G)**

- 1½ cups (338 g) dark brown sugar
- 1 cup (300 g) kosher salt
- 1 cup (96 g) coarsely ground black pepper
- 3 tablespoons (21 g) paprika
- 2 to 3 tablespoons (10 to 15 g) cayenne pepper, depending on heat preference
- 2 tablespoons (18 g) garlic powder
- 2 tablespoons (14 g) onion powder
- 1½ teaspoons ground turmeric
- 1½ teaspoons ginger powder

**Barbecue always needs a little sweetness, and this rub delivers just that. It's perfect for any cook where you're craving that classic sweet barbecue flavor. Adjust the cayenne to control the heat—whether you want a mild kick or a bolder spice. After the smoke, your meats will develop a beautiful brownish-red bark, balancing savory spices with that perfect touch of peppery sweetness.**

**1.** Combine the ingredients in a medium bowl and store in an airtight container in a cool, dark place. For best freshness, use within 4 to 6 months.

# CANDIED JALAPEÑOS

**MAKES ABOUT 2 CUPS (270 G)**

- ⅔ cup (158 ml) cider vinegar
- 2 cups (400 g) granulated sugar
- 1 pound (454 g) jalapeño peppers, sliced into ¼-inch (6-mm) rings
- Freshly grated zest of 2 limes
- Juice of 2 limes

**Once I started making these, they quickly became a staple in our fridge, right next to the pickled jalapeños. They're sweet, sure, but man, they pack a punch! Similar to hot honey, the chiles soak into the syrup, turning all that heat into something deep, flavorful, and seriously tasty. Toss a few of these into your sandwiches for that perfect balance of sweet heat. They go especially well with anything creamy, like coleslaw or layers of melty cheese.**

**1.** In a saucepan, combine the cider vinegar and sugar, then bring to a boil over medium heat. Reduce the heat to medium-low and stir to dissolve the sugar, letting it simmer for about 5 minutes.

**2.** Add the jalapeños and keep the liquid simmering, cooking until the peppers darken and start to wilt, about 4 to 5 minutes.

**3.** Using a slotted spoon, transfer the jalapeños to a glass jar (do not use plastic). Return the syrup to a gentle boil and cook for another 5 to 6 minutes, letting it reduce and thicken. Remove from the heat and stir in the lime zest and juice.

**4.** Carefully ladle the hot syrup into the jars with the jalapeños. Gently poke around with a fork to remove any air pockets between the peppers. Wipe the rim of the jar with a damp paper towel to remove any syrup, then seal the jar when it's cooled.

**5.** Let the jar rest in the fridge for a couple of days to develop the flavor before eating. Candied jalapeños will keep for about 2 months in the fridge.

# FRESH PICKLES

**MAKES 1 QUART (946 ML) JAR**

4 to 5 large pickling cucumbers

¼ cup (75 g) kosher salt, plus more as needed

2 sprigs fresh dill

2 cups (473 ml) water

2 cups (473 ml) distilled white vinegar

2 tablespoons (30 g) brown sugar

1 teaspoon mustard seeds

1 teaspoon ground turmeric

½ teaspoon black peppercorns

**OPTIONAL ADD-INS:**

Red pepper flakes

Bay leaf

Coriander seeds

Fennel seeds

**These pickles are a must for barbecue—not just for sandwiches, but for any kind of grilled or smoked meat. The crispy, tangy bite of pickles cuts through the rich, fatty flavors, and as the brine drips into the meat, it seasons it, bringing out the best flavors every time. This recipe uses salt to draw out moisture from the cucumbers before adding the brine, which makes them extra crispy. Depending on the size of your cucumbers, you may need to adjust the quantity or the brine, but the ratios will stay the same. Short on time? Try the Quick Pickles (p. 181). They're tasty and come together . . . quickly.**

**1.** Wash the cucumbers and cut them into slices about ⅛-inch (3-mm) thick.

**2.** Layer the cucumber slices in a small container, sprinkling the salt between each layer. Cover with plastic wrap and place a weight on top to help extract the water. Let it sit for 2 to 4 hours at room temperature.

**3.** Afterward, pour off the liquid and rinse the cucumbers under cold running water, tossing gently to remove the salt. Taste and adjust, then layer them in paper towels and let them dry. Don't use a salad spinner or you might bruise the cucumbers. Once dry, pack the cucumbers into a clean mason jar, placing the fresh dill at the bottom.

**4.** Put the water, vinegar, sugar, and spices in a pan over medium heat and stir until the sugar has dissolved. Carefully pour the warm liquid into the mason jar, fully covering the cucumbers. You may need to place a weight on top to submerge them in the brine. Allow the jar to cool before sealing it with a lid and storing it in the fridge. The pickles will develop more flavor after 2 to 3 days, so try to wait before digging in.

**Note:** This brine works especially well for English cucumbers, celery, carrots, chiles, cauliflower, okra, and fennel. Experiment with different combinations of sweeteners and vinegars to create exciting flavors. Vinegars vary in acidity, just as sweeteners vary in sweetness, so test out different combinations and adjust to suit your taste.

# QUICK PICKLES

**MAKES 1 PINT (473 ML) JAR**

2 English cucumbers
1 batch Master Brine (p. 181)
2 sprigs fresh dill
½ teaspoon black peppercorns
½ teaspoon chili flakes

**When you need pickles *now*, this is the recipe to grab. I usually prepare these while the meat's on the smoker, and they'll be ready in just a few hours, giving you that perfect tangy, sweet, and salty bite. If you've got fresh dill on hand, it'll make a big difference, but you can still pull this off with just the basic ingredients.**

**1.** Wash the cucumbers and cut them into thin slices about ⅛-inch (3-mm) thick. Pack the slices into a clean mason jar, placing the fresh dill at the bottom.

**2.** Carefully pour the warm brine into the mason jar, fully covering the cucumbers. You may need to place a weight on top to submerge them in the brine. Allow the jar to cool before sealing it with a lid and storing it in the fridge. The longer they rest, the more flavor they'll develop before serving.

## MASTER BRINE FOR QUICK PICKLING

**ABOUT 1 PINT (473 ML) JAR**

2 cups (473 ml) water
2 cups (473 ml) distilled white vinegar
2 tablespoons (26 g) white sugar
2 tablespoons (36 g) kosher salt

**OPTIONAL SUBSTITUTIONS:**
Apple cider vinegar
Rice wine vinegar
Brown sugar
Agave syrup
Maple syrup
Honey

**This is the baseline recipe that most of our pickling begins with. Depending on the flavor profile or type of pickle, spices and herbs can be added to create unique and exciting flavors. Check out the specific recipes in the following pages for some fun and tasty combinations that might inspire you as you craft your own delicious sandwiches.**

**1.** Warm up the ingredients in a pan over medium heat and stir until the salt and sugar has dissolved. Carefully pour the warm liquid into the mason jar, fully covering the fruits or vegetables of your choice. The pickles will be freshest within the first week.

# PICKLED JALAPEÑOS

**MAKES 1 PINT (473 ML) JAR**

- 8 to 10 jalapeños
- 1 bay leaf
- 1 clove garlic
- ½ teaspoon Mexican oregano
- ½ teaspoon dried thyme
- 1 batch Master Brine (p. 181)

**This is one of the most frequently made recipes in our house—I'm usually preparing a new batch every other week. We use them in all kinds of sandwiches, tacos, wraps, and sometimes just to top off scrambled eggs or nachos. The jalapeños are sweet, crisp, and have a nice tang from the brine, making them the perfect addition when you need that little extra punch between the layers.**

**1.** Wash the jalapeños and slice off the stems. Cut them into thin slices, about ⅛-inch (3-mm) thick. Place them in the jar along with the bay leaf, garlic, oregano, and thyme.

**2.** Carefully pour the warm brine into the mason jar, fully covering the jalapeños. You may need to place a weight on top to submerge them in the brine. Allow the jar to cool before sealing it with a lid and storing it in the fridge. Pickled jalapeños will stay good for up to 3 to 4 weeks, unless you eat them all first.

# PICKLED RED ONIONS

**MAKES 1 PINT (473 ML) JAR**

- 2 red onions
- 1 habanero, seeded and diced
- 2 garlic cloves
- 2 cups (473 ml) water
- 1 cup (235 ml) distilled white vinegar
- 1 cup (235 ml) apple cider vinegar
- 2 tablespoons (26 g) white sugar
- 2 tablespoons (36 g) kosher salt
- 1 tablespoon (3 g) Mexican oregano
- ½ teaspoon black peppercorns

**Tangy red onions are the perfect pairing for any barbecue with Southwest, Mediterranean, and Middle Eastern flavors—each culinary region has its own version of pickled or marinated red onions. Make a batch of these to add a touch of sweet heat from the habanero, which is just spicy enough to give you a little kick. The pickling process mellows out the heat, leaving them with the perfect spicy zing to top your meats.**

**1.** You can slice the red onions into thin strips or rings—whichever you prefer. Slice the onions to about ⅛-inch (3-mm) thickness and place the slices into a clean mason jar along with the finely diced habanero and garlic.

**2.** Warm up the rest of the ingredients in a pan over medium heat and stir until the salt and sugar has dissolved. Carefully pour the warm liquid into the mason jar, fully covering the onions. You may need to place a weight on top to submerge them in the brine. Allow the jar to cool before sealing it with a lid and storing it in the fridge. The longer they rest, the more flavor they'll develop before serving.

# PICKLED BRUSSELS SPROUTS

**MAKES 1 TO 2 PINT (473 TO 946 ML) JARS**

- 20 to 24 Brussels sprouts
- 2 sprigs fresh dill
- 2 cups (473 ml) water
- 1½ cups (355 ml) distilled white vinegar
- ½ cup (188 ml) rice wine vinegar
- 2 tablespoons (26 g) white sugar
- 2 tablespoons (36 g) kosher salt
- 1 teaspoon chili flakes
- 1 teaspoon mustard seeds
- ½ teaspoon black peppercorns

**If you're looking for a crunchy, tangy bite with a little funk, these pickled vegetables are your go-to. These sprouts offer the same bold, tangy punch as sauerkraut or kimchi, but with a distinct flavor and texture that make them stand out on any sandwich. The crispy texture and bold flavor are perfect for pairing with hearty sandwiches like my Smoked Pastrami Steak (p. 37) or Smoked Brat Burgers (p. 55). I love customizing them with extra chiles for some heat or going classic with a big punch of dill. The best part? You get to decide how you want them. Slice them up and you've got the perfect sandwich topper.**

**1.** Wash the Brussels sprouts and trim the ends. Depending on the size of them, you may need to slice them in half. Fit them in the jar and determine how many can be packed in, then trim as needed. They will need a little space between them to allow the liquid to surround them.

**2.** Place the fresh dill in the clean mason jar and pack in the trimmed Brussels sprouts.

**3.** Warm up the other ingredients in a pan over medium heat and stir until the salt and sugar has dissolved. Carefully pour the warm liquid into the mason jar, fully covering the Brussels. You may need to place a weight on top to submerge them in the brine. Allow the jar to cool before sealing it with a lid and storing it in the fridge. The longer they rest, the more flavor they'll develop before serving.

**Note:** Brussels sprouts, like sauerkraut and kimchi, will produce $CO_2$, so be sure to "burp" the jar every couple of days after pickling to release the pressure.

# PICKLED OKRA

**MAKES 1 PINT (473 ML) JAR**

- 1 pound (454 g) fresh okra
- 1 tablespoon (4 g) chili flakes
- 1 teaspoon celery seeds
- 1 teaspoon dried thyme
- ½ teaspoon black peppercorns
- 2 cups (473 ml) water
- 2 cups (437 ml) distilled white vinegar
- 1 tablespoon (13 g) white sugar
- 2 tablespoons (36 g) kosher salt

**Crunchy and sour pickled okra has just the right amount of zing to balance out spicy Southern dishes like the Cajun Chicken Sandwich (p. 29) or Cajun Bayou Dip (p. 97). Not only are they great straight out of the jar, but they're hearty enough to skewer and grill as a crispy topping or be diced up for a coleslaw with some real punch. You'll want to keep a jar of these on hand.**

**1.** Pack as many okra pods as you can into the jar, with the tips pointing up. Sprinkle in the chili flakes, celery seeds, thyme, and peppercorns. Finish packing the jar with more okra, tips pointing down, filling in the gaps between the pods.

**2.** Warm the water, vinegar, sugar, and salt in a pan over medium heat, stirring until the salt and sugar dissolve. Carefully pour the warm liquid into the mason jar, completely covering the okra and leaving about ¼ inch (6 mm) of space at the top.

**3.** Allow the jar to cool before sealing with a lid and storing it in the fridge. Let the pickles rest for at least 2 days before serving, as they'll develop better flavor during this time.

# ACKNOWLEDGMENTS

**I AM TRULY GRATEFUL** for the opportunity to write this second cookbook and share my ideas and experiences with the world. It's humbling to know that people are interested in my story and creations. I'm passionate about teaching, and I hope this book inspires many to get out in their backyard and cook more.

Barbecue is all about service and community, and I want to start by giving my deepest thanks to the Lord. He has blessed me with the opportunity, wisdom, and determination to write this book, and I'm excited to use my gifts to help others serve their families and friends.

A huge thank you to my family, especially my wife, Yarizeth. Her patience and unwavering belief in my vision has been a constant source of strength. She sacrificed her time to make sure I had everything I needed to bring this book to life. I also want to thank my two boys, Braxton and Zachariah, for their endless enthusiasm and excitement about every single recipe. I hope you keep that curiosity and joy as you grow.

To my neighbors and community—thank you for being my taste testers! It's been a blast walking my sandwiches across the street and down the block to share them with you. Your feedback has been invaluable.

Thank you to my close friends Steve and Kathy Jang. Not only did you help me by consuming many sandwiches, but you also extended mental and parental support, helping out with our kids and giving me that extra time when I needed it the most.

To my close friend, Jason Raducha, and his team at Noble Bread, an artisan bakery in Phoenix, Arizona: I've had so much fun learning about the hand-crafted quality breads you produce. Our partnership has transformed the way I look at sandwiches, and I'm grateful for the hours of brainstorming, joking, learning, and, of course, the many, many loaves of bread you've donated to the cause. I couldn't have created this cookbook without your local support.

To my unofficial editor and partner in crime, Nicole Stover: Your willingness to dive into my drafts and mark them up with plenty of red ink helped me communicate more clearly and authentically. I'm so grateful for your unwavering support.

To my close friends and fellow recipe creators—thank you for checking in on me and making sure I still have a pulse! I truly appreciate the long talks, brainstorming sessions, and continuous encouragement. Writing a book is no simple task, and it's rare to find close friends who truly understand the many hats that come with it. Special thanks to Colin Barker, Derek Wolf, Heather Scholten, and Christie Vanover—your friendship and support have been immeasurable.

And lastly, thank you to my dedicated readers from Chiles and Smoke. Your excitement and encouragement from the first cookbook stoked my fire and passion, fueling more creative ideas along the way. I truly appreciate all of you—you're the biggest reason I'm able to do this.

# ABOUT THE AUTHOR

**BRAD PROSE** is a professional recipe developer, food writer, cookbook author, and culinary photographer. He is the founder and force behind Chiles and Smoke, a website dedicated to inspiring readers to use new flavor combinations, techniques, and ingredients when grilling or smoking. His combined passion for fine dining and BBQ shines through his presentations and cooking style. Making his mark in the wide world of BBQ, Brad produces high-quality, unique recipes to challenge and expand the home cook's comfort zone. He has cooked on *LIVE with Kelly and Ryan* and has published recipes in BBQGuys, *Tailgater Magazine*, and many other publications. He is also the author of the book *Chiles and Smoke*. You can keep up to date with his work on social media and on his website: chilesandsmoke.com.

# INDEX

**D**



**E**



**F**



**G**



**H**

**I**



**J**



**K**



**L**



**M**